CULTURES OF THE WORLD®

BOSNIA AND HERZEGOVINA

David C. King

BENCHMARK **B**OOKS

MARSHALL CAVENDISH
NEW YORK

PICTURE CREDITS

Cover photo: © Susan Hill/Art Directors

AFP: 119, 121, 125 • alt.TYPE/REUTERS: 10, 13, 31, 36, 38, 39, 56, 65, 67, 75, 79, 82, 85, 91, 98, 99, 101, 102, 120 • ANA Press Agency: 32, 54, 76 • Bob Battersby/Eye Ubiquitous: 87, 111, 124 • Robert Bremac: 88 • Corbis Inc.: 17, 18, 22, 24, 25, 26, 27, 35, 47, 48, 50, 51, 55, 60, 73, 77, 78, 80, 81, 84, 92, 93, 95, 97, 100, 105, 115, 122, 123, 127, 128 • John Dakers/Eye Ubiquitous: 86 • Melanie Friend/Hutchison Library: 64, 68 • HBL Network Photo Agency: 3, 4, 11, 12, 14, 15, 28, 29, 33, 34, 40, 43, 46, 53, 57, 58, 59, 70, 72, 83, 112, 116 • Juliet Highet /Hutchison Library: 44, 106, 107, 108 • Crispin Hughes/Hutchison Library: 61, 62, 69, 74, 110 • International Photobank: 6, 7, 8, 16, 41, 45, 66, 94, 103, 104, 113, 118 • Victoria Ivleva-Yorke/Hutchison Library: 49 • Lonely Planet Images: 9, 23, 63, 126 • MC Picture Library: 129 • Liz McLeod/Hutchison Library: 114 • North Wind Picture Archives: 19, 21 • Stephen Pern/Hutchison Library: 42, 52 • Sylvia Cordaiy Photo Library: 1, 5, 109 • Vanda Tea: 130 • Audrius Tomonis/www.banknotes.com: 135 • TopFoto: 96, 117 • Gary Trotter/Eye Ubiquitous: 37 • Richard Wareham: 30, 71 • Bernhard Winkelmann/StockFood: 130

ACKNOWLEDGMENTS

Thanks to Gordon N. Bardos, Assistant Director, Harriman Institute, Columbia University, for his expert reading of this manuscript.

PRECEDING PAGE

Bosnian children have fun snowsledding in their country's mountains in winter. The capital, Sarajevo, hosted the Winter Olympic Games in 1984.

Marshall Cavendish
99 White Plains Road
Tarrytown, NY 10591
Website: www.marshallcavendish.us

© Marshall Cavendish International (Asia) Private Limited 2005
® "Cultures of the World" is a registered trademark of Marshall Cavendish Corporation.

Series concept and design by Times Editions
An imprint of Marshall Cavendish International (Asia) Private Limited
A member of Times Publishing Limited

Library of Congress Cataloging-in-Publication Data
King, David C.
  Bosnia and Herzegovina / David C. King.— 1st ed.
    p. cm. — (Cultures of the world)
  Summary: "Explores the geography, history, government, economy, people, and culture of Bosnia and Herzegovina"—Provided by publisher.
  Includes bibliographical references and index.
  ISBN 0-7614-1853-9
  1. Bosnia and Herzegovina—Juvenile literature. I. Title. II. Series.
  DR1660.K56 2005
  949.742—dc22   2004021120

Printed in China

7 6 5 4 3 2 1

CONTENTS

Saudi Arabia financed the construction of the Kralj Fahd bin Abdul Aziz Al Saud mosque in Alipasino Polje, Sarajevo.

**A lady casts her vote in a
Bosnian election.**

INTRODUCTION

IN 1984 THE CITY OF Sarajevo, capital of Bosnia and Herzegovina, was the proud host of the Winter Olympic Games, and the world wondered at the beauty and peacefulness of this small mountainous country on the Balkan Peninsula. Even more impressive was the fact that people of very different backgrounds and religions were living peacefully together. Roman Catholic Croats were friends and neighbors of Muslim Slavs and of Eastern Orthodox Serbs.

Only eight years after the closing ceremonies of the Olympics, Bosnia and Herzegovina exploded in a bloody and bitter three-way civil war. Four years of fighting ended only with the intervention of a United Nations force that included 8,000 U.S. troops. The war devastated Sarajevo and the country, but the people have shown a remarkable resilience and determination. The rebuilding includes the restoration of ancient churches and mosques as people heal deep ethnic and religious conflicts.

GEOGRAPHY

THE MOUNTAINS AND HILLS of Bosnia and Herzegovina are wedged between the nations of Serbia and Montenegro on the east and Croatia on the north, west, and south. The entire Balkan Peninsula—which Bosnia and the other two countries share with Romania, Bulgaria, Slovenia, Albania, Macedonia, Greece, and Turkey—was a region of turmoil and strife through most of the 20th century. An assassination in the capital city of Sarajevo was the spark that touched off World War I (1914–18); much of the guerilla warfare of World War II (1939–45) took place here; and a three-way civil war devastated Bosnia-Herzegovina and its neighbors.

Covering an area of 19,735 square miles (51,129 square km), this rugged country is slightly larger than Vermont and New Hampshire combined. And as in those two U.S. states, the mountains of Bosnia have fostered a fierce spirit of independence while also making it difficult for any outside power either to invade or to control pockets of resistance.

The Dinaric Alps form both a physical barrier and a state boundary between Bosnia and Croatia. This gives Croatia control of the Dalmatian coast and leaves Bosnia-Herzegovina almost completely landlocked, with only about a 12-mile (19-km) coastline on the Adriatic Sea. The Dinaric Alps, and smaller ranges extending east from them, are on geological fault lines, which leads to occasional earthquakes. One earthquake in 1969 destroyed more than half the buildings in Banja Luka city. Another, much smaller earthquake was ironic in its timing—striking Sarajevo in 1992, the year the civil war erupted.

Above: **The Turkish Quarter is a lively marketplace that is full of restaurants, cafés, and shops.**

Opposite: **A view of Mostar city and the Neretva River that runs through it.**

The Una River.

MOUNTAINS AND RIVER VALLEYS

The mountain ranges that stretch east from the Dinaric Alps include some of the most rugged and tallest mountains on the Balkan Peninsula. The highest point in the country is Mount Maglic at 7,831 feet (2,387 m), located near the eastern border with Montenegro.

The mountainous terrain makes transportation difficult, and there are few east-west roads. Over the centuries Bosnians settled the fertile river valleys, most of them flowing north into the Sava River, a tributary of the Danube, which also forms the northern border with Croatia. North-flowing rivers in Bosnia-Herzegovina include the Bosna, Drina, Una, and Vrbas. In the south, the Neretva is the only major river that carves its way through the Dinarics and across Croatia, flowing west to the Adriatic.

The city of Mostar is located on the Neretva River in a fertile area of cypress and fig trees that is like an oasis within the barren karst landscape. The Sava River valley, along with the valleys of the other rivers flowing into it, provide most of Bosnia's best farmland. Although these fertile valleys make up less than 15 percent of the land area, they make farming and raising livestock a major part of the country's economy.

THE KARST LANDSCAPE

The limestone outcroppings known as a karst region *(below)* are found in other parts of Europe as well as in Asia and parts of the United States, but the name was first used to describe parts of Bosnia-Herzegovina and Slovenia. Large areas of these plateaus have deep faults, or cracks, and jagged ravines. These ravines form as rain dissolves softer portions of the limestone, leading to the creation of countless caves and underground streams. When the ceiling of a cave is close to the surface, it may collapse, forming a sinkhole—a phenomenon that occurs in parts of the United States as well.

In parts of Herzegovina, several depressions may join together to form a *polje* (POLE-jeh)—a narrow field where enough soft limestone has eroded to produce soil suitable for some crops or for grazing. Streams that overflow their banks in winter and spring deposit additional rich soil. One *polje* near Mostar is nearly 40 miles (64 km) long and is called Popo Polje, the Priest's Valley, because it was once church-owned.

The so-called rock rivers—streams that gush out of the side of a mountain and then often disappear underground again—are another unusual feature of the karst landscapes. The same river may surface then disappear several times. Underground caves are also interconnected in ways that are not visible on the surface. Shepherds report seeing flocks of sheep disappear into a cave and then emerge from another cave some distance away.

CLIMATE

Bosnians cool off from the summer heat at a fountain in Sarajevo. During Bosnia's civil war, hundreds of millions of dollars' worth of damages were inflicted on the water system, which will take years to rebuild to its pre-war efficiency.

The jagged Dinaric Alps have a strong influence on the climate of Bosnia-Herzegovina. The Adriatic Sea, for example, like other coastal waters, has a moderating influence on the climate, usually producing milder winters and cool summers. But the Dinarics block the influence of the sea's currents, so they affect Croatia's Dalmatian coast, but not the interior of Bosnia. Differences in atmospheric pressure between the air above the mountains and the air over the Adriatic produce strong winds—including cold bora, or *yougo* (YOU-goh), winds that move from north to south. The result is that Bosnia-Herzegovina has a modified Continental climate, with

warm summers and cold winters. But a Mediterranean climate prevails in the south with sunny, warm summers and mild, rainy winters.

Temperatures and precipitation levels are also influenced by the mountains. Mostar, on the Neretva River and near the Adriatic Sea, has an average January temperature of 43°F (6°C), while Banja Luka in the north is 11°F cooler (32°F/0°C). Because of the wind patterns, the north receives its heaviest precipitation in the summer; while in the south, rainfall is heaviest in autumn and winter.

The best time to observe the beauty of Bosnia-Herzegovina is in springtime, when most of the country experiences mild conditions, although areas at higher elevations might still be covered with snow.

Winters in Bosnia-Herzegovina are bitterly cold, and temperatures can dip as low as 25°F (-4°C).

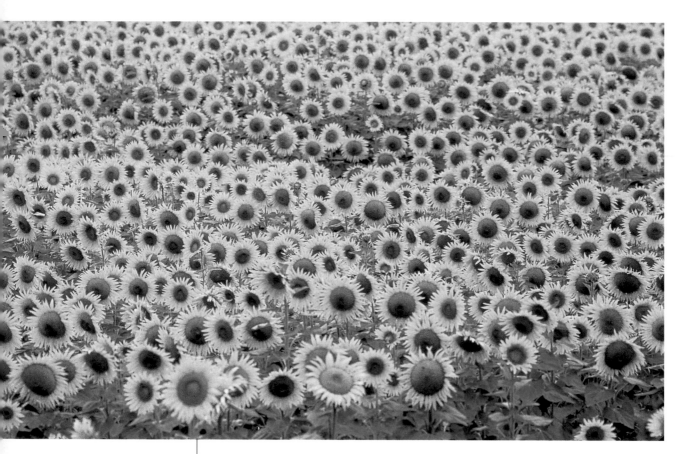

FLORA

News reports of the civil war of the 1990s and of the UN peacekeeping force gave Americans daily television images of Bosnia's spectacular mountains, with their dense forests of beech, oak, and pine. The forests have made lumbering and furniture-making important parts of the country's economy.

Bosnia-Herzegovina has a surprising variety of plant life. One reason for this is that the mountains have protected some plant species from becoming extinct due to human activity and the invasion of other plant types. Some preserved species date from the ice ages, making the fertile valleys of the north a favorite area for scientists studying the evolution of certain rare species. About 20 percent of the plant species identified here are not found growing wild anywhere else in the world. Botanists are most fascinated by the types of trees, such as the horse chestnut, a tree that is descended from the rich plant life of the Tertiary period, some 65 million years ago.

Several kinds of shrubs that are now common in the gardens and yards of Europe and North America were spread from western Asia by way of Bosnia. Lilacs, for instance, were introduced by the Ottoman Turks in the 16th century. The shrubs then made their way to Vienna, and from there to western Europe.

The Asian variety of forsythia followed a similar route. Through careful selection, the shrub and its blossoms in the North American varieties are larger than those in the Balkans.

MEDICINAL PLANTS Wild plants have been collected for healing purposes for centuries, and scientists are now analyzing them for possible applications in modern medicine.

Lungwort, for example, has long been used by rural healers to ease breathing problems, as the name implies; pharmaceutical companies are now using it in asthma medicines.

Similarly, wild plantain, which is a common roadside weed used in folk remedies, has been found useful for some digestive disorders and as a cough remedy.

FAUNA

Bosnia's countless limestone caves, particularly in the north, provide habitat for a variety of unusual animals. Cave spiders, crickets, and several kinds of millipedes are fascinating to scientists studying how animals adapt to environmental conditions.

One recent discovery was the *proteus*, or *olm*—an almost colorless creature, similar to the salamander, that has lived in the complete darkness of the caves for so long that it has no eyes.

The mountains, forests, lakes, and streams of Bosnia-Herzegovina have drawn hunters and fishers for several centuries. Even after war's destruction and the loss of habitat to lumbering, farming, and pollution, that lure remains at the start of the 21st century. More than one-third of the country's land area is forested, especially on the lower slopes of the hills and mountains. Hunters are drawn by a variety of wild game—wolves, bears, chamois, deers, otters, and boars. Animal migrations to more spacious habitat in Romania and Bulgaria have severely reduced the numbers of such animals in Bosnia. Those that remain are still targeted by hunters.

Other wildlife in Bosnia-Herzegovina include

fox, wolf, badger, and wildcat, as well as birds of prey, such as eagle, buzzard, hawk, and vulture. A wide variety of birds populate the Balkan region, ranging from tiny warblers and wrens to storks, cranes, herons, and geese. In spite of environmental problems, such as acid rain, many glacial lakes and swift mountain streams still provide trout, bass, and many other game fish.

Hutovo Blato National Park in southern Herzegovina provides shelter for more than 240 bird species as well as other small and large animals. The waters of the park are full of eel, carp, and other freshwater fish. This park was once a popular hunting spot. While hunting is still permitted, so-called photo safaris are now heavily promoted.

Opposite: **In Bosnia-Herzegovina certain species of wolves, such as the gray wolf, are unprotected and declining in number due to hunting.**

Below: **A mountain goat surveys the landscape.**

HISTORY

LITTLE IS KNOWN OF the earliest people who lived in what is now Bosnia-Herzegovina. Historians refer to all of eastern Europe in the years from 7000 B.C. to 3500 B.C. simply as Old Europe. Groups of people settled into a farming life and some of the groups in the Balkan Peninsula achieved the earliest civilization in Europe, probably building on ideas carried north from Greece. These little-known people mined copper and later iron, created sophisticated ceramics, and had organized government, religion, and some form of writing.

About the 10th century B.C. people called Illyrians moved into the Balkan Peninsula from Asia Minor (modern Turkey) and continued the high level of civilization. In 228 B.C. the queen of the Illyrians, Teuta, caused so much turmoil by her conquests that powerful Roman armies moved in, finally took control in 33 B.C., and transformed the western Balkan Peninsula into a province called Illyricum.

For several hundred years the province enjoyed great prosperity and served as a major buffer between the Roman Empire and the tribes of northern "barbarians"—societies like the Goths and Huns—who constantly pressured the empire.

Illyricum was so important to Rome that many of the late emperors were Illyrians, chosen by their soldiers, including Diocletian (who lived from A.D. 245 to 316 and reigned for 21 years) and Constantine the Great. During the late Roman years many people in the province were converted to Christianity, giving their allegiance to the church in Rome, which became the Roman Catholic Church.

Above: **Constantine the Great was the first Roman emperor who became a Christian. He lived from A.D. 280 to 237.**

Opposite: **The Ottoman Turks built the Stari Most bridge in the 16th century.**

17

ROMAN CONQUESTS

The Roman conquest, along with the pressure of people moving in from the north, established a pattern for the region that was to continue for the next 2,000 years. One part of the pattern was the movement of different groups into present-day Bosnia-Herzegovina. At the same time, powerful empires attempted to gain control of the entire region.

Both parts of the pattern were influenced by the rugged mountain ranges. Outside invaders, for example, could not prevent independent bands from continuing their resistance from their strongholds high up in the mountains. At the same time, however, migrating groups searching for a place to settle could find their way through narrow passes into the fertile river valleys.

MIGRATIONS

One of the most powerful forces shaping history was the migration of the people called "barbarians" from Asia westward across the plains of Russia and Poland, which spread into every corner of Europe. Dozens of migrating societies—Goths, Visigoths, Huns, Angles, Saxons, Danes, and others—swept into Europe, often conquering and destroying until they,

too, settled and adopted civilized ways. By the fifth century A.D., Goths, Visigoths, Huns, and others had forced the Romans to divide the empire into West and East, with the Eastern Empire becoming known as the Byzantine Empire. Even that did not prevent the complete collapse of the Western Roman Empire.

During the sixth and seventh centuries, warlike Slavic tribes moved into the Balkans. The groups that settled in what is now Bosnia were the Croats and the Serbs, or South Slavs.

Another new influence entered the region during the eighth and ninth centuries A.D. as the Byzantine Empire tried to gain control. This new civilization added a rich and varied culture to what is now Bosnia-Herzegovina, including striking achievements in art, architecture, and literature. Byzantium also sent two monks, Cyril and Methodius, who succeeded in converting many Serbs to the Eastern Orthodox Church—the Eastern branch of the Christian church. Other Serbs and most Croats remained in the Roman Catholic Church.

Above: **The Huns were nomads. They were one of the groups of people who migrated from Asia to Europe in A.D. 370.**

Opposite: **A Roman cavalryman on horseback. Roman conquests began toward the end of the fifth century B.C.**

Opposite: **In 1453 Ottomans conquered the Byzantine Empire and made Constantinople the capital of the new Ottoman Empire. In 1463 their rule expanded to what was to become Bosnia-Herzegovina.**

THE KINGDOM OF BOSNIA

The demographic makeup of modern Bosnia-Herzegovina was now taking shape: Roman Catholic Croats occupied much of the north, while Serbs in the south were divided—some Catholic and some members of the Eastern Church. Differences in language and the alphabet were also introduced.

Geographic lines also became clearer around A.D. 900 when a new kingdom, called Bosnia, emerged near the source of the Bosna River. Independence was soon limited when the powerful Kingdom of Hungary tried to control large areas of the Balkans.

From the late 1100s to 1463, the Hungarians appointed viceroys called *bans* (BAHNS) to rule Bosnia. In the 14th century, one of the most powerful bans, Stjepan Kotromani, added the territory of Hum—later renamed Herzegovina—to Bosnia. The two have remained connected ever since.

Under another strong *ban*, King Tvrtko I, who ruled from 1353 to 1391, Bosnia-Herzegovina, then the most powerful state in the Balkans, enjoyed a brief golden age. Although Kotromani and Tvrtko technically ruled as Hungarian viceroys, their reigns are considered the greatest period of Bosnia-Herzegovina's early history.

THE OTTOMAN TURKS

At various times from about 900 to 1463, other outside powers tried to take control of Bosnia-Herzegovina. The city-state of Venice as well as Serbia, Croatia, and Hungary all competed for control. None managed to conquer the region.

Then, in 1463 another powerful empire moved in—the Ottoman Turks. From their base in Turkey, the Ottoman rulers took control of the Muslim empire. The Muslims, followers of the religion of Islam, had built a great empire that stretched from the western Mediterranean across southern Asia to present-day Indonesia. The empire stretched west across northern Africa into Spain.

As the Byzantine Empire weakened and collapsed in the early 1400s the Ottoman rulers took over much of the area the Byzantines had controlled. Islam had become one of the world's great religions and had also achieved a high level of civilization, leading the world for several centuries in science, mathematics, architecture, and medicine, with great achievements also in art and literature.

During the 15th and 16th centuries, as the Ottoman Turkish rulers solidified their control over Bosnia-Herzegovina, many Bosnians converted to Islam. With the addition of the Muslim influence, Bosnia now had the ethnic, religious, and cultural mix that characterizes the country today.

There were now three main groups. Bosnian Muslims, also known as Bosniaks, are today the largest group. The second largest group is the Serbs, who belong to the Eastern Orthodox Church, followed by the Croats, most of whom are Roman Catholic.

NATIONALISM AND WAR

The 18th and 19th centuries were a period of intense nationalism throughout the world. People in a geographic area who shared a common language, culture, and history longed for nationhood—a nation-state that would allow them to control their own destiny.

This powerful impulse was involved in the creation of the United States in the 18th century and in the independence movements of Latin America in the early 1800s, as well as in Greece, Germany, and Italy a little later. This nationalist spirit rocked the Balkan Peninsula, too. After going through frequent wars, plagues, repeated invasions by Austria, and uprisings by the locals, Bosnia-Herzegovina succeeded in breaking away from the Ottoman Empire in 1875 and became a protectorate of the Austro-Hungarian empire three years later.

Archduke Franz Ferdinand on a visit to Sarajevo, just hours before his assassination.

By 1900 a larger nationalist movement called Pan-Slavism swept eastern Europe. This was a desire to unite all Slavic peoples, including the Slavs living in Bosnia, Serbia, Poland, and Russia. The rulers of Austria-Hungary hoped to stall this movement by annexing Bosnia and Herzegovina in 1908.

The nationalist drive continued to gain strength, especially the desire to create an independent Slavic state limited to the Balkans. It was to be called Yugoslavia—the land of the South Slavs. On June 28, 1914, when the heir to the Austro-Hungarian throne visited Sarajevo, a few Yugoslav nationalists saw a chance to strike a blow for their cause. The royal visitor—the Archduke Franz Ferdinand—and his wife, Sophie, were shot dead by a Bosnian Serb named Gavrilo Princip.

A worker restores the bridge where Austro-Hungarian Archduke Franz Ferdinand was assassinated in 1914. His death sparked off World War I.

The assassination turned out to be one of the momentous events of the 20th century. Austria-Hungary declared war on Serbia, and Russia responded by rushing to the aid of Slavic Serbia. Several interlocking treaties quickly went into effect and, in August 1914, Europe and much of the world were plunged into the Great War (1914–18), later called, simply, World War I.

Following the horror of the war, the first to witness the use of modern weapons such as airplanes, submarines, tanks, machine guns, and poison gas, the leaders of the victorious Allies redrew the map of Europe in the Treaty of Versailles. Both the Ottoman Empire and the Austro-Hungarian empire were broken up, and an attempt was made to create new boundaries that would satisfy nationalist ambitions. Bosnia was included in the Kingdom of Serbs, Croats, and Slovenes; in 1929 the name was changed to Yugoslavia.

WOODROW WILSON'S FOURTEEN POINTS

The United States entered World War I in 1917, and the addition of 2 million U.S. troops, plus weapons, food, and other supplies, enabled the Allied powers, led by Great Britain and France, to defeat the Central powers (Germany and Austria-Hungary). In leading the United States into the war, President Woodrow Wilson proposed Fourteen Points as the basis for peace *(below)*. One of the major points was called the right of self-determination—that is, the right of the people to choose or create their own nation.

The principle was applied to the former empires, but it was impossible to draw national boundaries that would satisfy every group. On the positive side, Wilson's idea led to the creation of Yugoslavia. But within the new federation and throughout the Balkans, the spirit of nationalism had not been fully satisfied, and trouble would flare again in the 1990s.

FIFTY YEARS AS YUGOSLAVIA

In 1939, 20 years after Yugoslavia was formed, Nazi Germany and other military dictatorships again drove the world into war—World War II (1939 –45). Early in the war, Nazi troops marched into Yugoslavia. In the north, they created a puppet government called the Independent State of Croatia, which included Bosnia-Herzegovina. The Germans allowed the Croatian fascist organization, Ustasa, to do as they pleased with the ethnic and religious minorities of Bosnia. The Ustasa killed an estimated 100,000 Serbs and sent more than 14,000 Jews to gas chambers in the Nazi death camps. Thousands of Bosnian men and women resisted the Ustasa forces by joining Yugoslav guerrillas in the mountains. The guerrillas, called Partisans, were led by Josip Broz, better known as Marshal Tito. His leadership, combined with supplies from the Allies and the fierce determination of the Partisans, made this the most effective guerrilla force in all of Europe. They forced the Germans out of the country before the war ended in 1945, and Tito was made head of the new government.

Yugoslavian prisoners of war look sullenly at their Nazi captors, who invaded the country during World War II.

COMMUNIST RULE Under Tito, Yugoslavia became a Communist state and enjoyed 45 years of peace. Postwar Yugoslavia was made up of six republics—Bosnia-Herzegovina, Croatia, Slovenia, Serbia, Macedonia, and Montenegro, plus two Serbian provinces—Kosovo and Vojvodina. Although Tito enjoyed friendly relations with the Soviet Union, he managed to keep Yugoslavia out of Soviet control. In spite of heavy pressure from Moscow, Tito managed to steer an independent course, while most other Communist countries fell under the control of the Soviet Union. In the 1980s the weaknesses of Communism were becoming apparent in the growing economic stagnation. This led to a resurgence of nationalistic spirits. Tito's death in 1980 removed the one person who might have held the federation together. By the late 1980s the Communist structures throughout Europe were beginning to break apart, including the Soviet Union and Yugoslavia.

Visiting Yugoslavian president Tito and his wife (*second and first from right*) ride with three Russian leaders in an open car as they arrive at an exhibition near Moscow in 1956.

TITO—DICTATOR OF UNITY

From 1945 until his death in 1980, the man known to the world as Marshal Tito *(right)* ruled the six federated republics of Yugoslavia with an iron hand. As long as Tito was in power, a tight lid was kept on the bitter ethnic and religious feuds that had been seething for decades.

He was born Josip Broz on May 7, 1892, the seventh of 15 children born to a poor peasant family in Croatia. He became a metal worker and mechanic, working in Austria, and fought in the Austrian army in World War I (1914–18). He was wounded, captured by the Russians, and sent to a prisoner-of-war camp where he learned about Communism. After the war, he became active in the Communist Party of Yugoslavia (KPJ), although the government was trying to suppress all Communist organizations. Broz was sentenced to five years in prison for his communist activities and, in 1934 began working underground, adopting the alias of Tito.

In 1941, when German troops invaded Yugoslavia, Tito organized the Communist partisan resistance movement. Although the Allies, including the United States, were reluctant to cooperate with a Communist movement, they soon realized that Tito led the most effective resistance forces, not only in Yugoslavia but anywhere in Europe. Finally furnished with weapons and supplies, Tito's partisans kept Hitler's armies and Croatian allies from gaining control of the country, although Tito was seriously wounded and nearly captured twice in surprise raids.

As the war drew to a close in 1945, Tito consolidated his power. He ignored the government-in-exile in England and simply took control. He abolished the monarchy and made the Federal Republic of Yugoslavia a one-party state. Throughout the years of the Cold War, he refused to surrender any control to the Soviet-dominated Communist bloc countries, nor would he cooperate with the U.S.-led Free World. Instead, Tito steered an independent course and joined other nonaligned nations, including Egypt and China.

Within Yugoslavia, Tito's word remained the law. In 1953 he was named president of Yugoslavia as well as prime minister, and in 1974 he became president for life. The personal qualities that enabled Tito to remain in power so long included his immense stamina, an ability to adapt to changed conditions, and decisiveness once he chose a direction. He had a lively sense of humor and enjoyed life to the fullest, traveling widely, marrying three times, and pursuing his hobbies—hunting, fishing, and photography. He was also an excellend pianist and was said to be one of Europe's best-dressed leaders.

The importance of Tito's dictatorship became clear in the years following his death in 1980. The Communist control of the country weakened and the long-suppressed rivalries and hatreds soon splintered the country and led to civil war.

The civil war caused wide-spread devastation in Mostar, a southern city.

THE CIVIL WAR YEARS

The breakup of the Communist regime in Yugoslavia began in 1991, when Croatia, Slovenia, and Macedonia all declared their independence. The Serb-dominated Yugoslav army immediately moved in to crush the independence movements. When Bosnia declared its independence the following March, Serbs in Bosnia-Herzegovina saw a chance to take control of the country; they formed an army and asked the Yugoslav army to help. Many Croats, fearing that they would be dominated in a Muslim-controlled Bosnia, joined in the fighting against the Bosniaks, making it a three-sided civil war.

The war was ugly, bloody, and bitter. The generations of peace among the different religious groups was buried beneath an avalanche of violence. The Bosnian Serbs, supported by the Yugoslav army, surrounded the once-vibrant capital of Sarajevo and began pounding it with artillery and rocket fire, slowly reducing it to rubble simply because it was primarily a Muslim city. More than 10,000 Sarajevans were killed by artillery and

sniper fire, and more than 50,000 were wounded. The Serbs attacked other Muslim cities and towns, crowding thousands into concentration camps and burying thousands more in mass graves. These wholesale murders and atrocities were known as the policy of ethnic cleansing—an effort to destroy or drive away all non-Serbs, much like Hitler's policy of genocide against Jews before and during World War II. For years after the war, mass graves continued to be discovered, including one in September 2003 that contained an estimated 500 bodies.

At the start of the civil war, Croat forces took part in the attacks on Bosniaks, but the Croats soon found that the Serbs were quite as willing to kill Croats as Muslims. Consequently, in 1994 the Croats agreed to a cease-fire with Bosniaks and joined forces with the Bosnian army. At the same time, as news of the Serbs' ethnic cleansing spread, world opinion condemned the atrocities, and the United Nations (UN) launched an investi-gation into possible war crimes. The UN also sent in a peacekeeping force, but it had little success at first.

The United Nations sent troops to Bosnia-Herzegovina in 1994 to help with the delivery of humanitarian aid and for peacekeeping purposes.

Throughout Sarajevo there are scars in the pavement—indentations that look something like a skeletal hand. The marks were caused by exploding shells during the siege. People call them Sarajevo Roses, and have filled in some of them with red paint, symbolizing the blood shed during the conflict in the city.

NATO INTERVENTION By 1995 the Bosniak-Croat alliance began to win battles, although the Serbs still controlled roughly two-thirds of the country. Late in August, with UN support, the North Atlantic Treaty Organization (NATO) launched a series of air strikes, led by American and British jets, against Serbian targets. This quickly persuaded the Serb leaders to lift the siege of Sarajevo and agree to truce talks.

At the invitation of U.S. President Bill Clinton, negotiations were held in Dayton, Ohio, in November 1995, producing an agreement that was signed in Paris on December 14, 1995. The Dayton Agreement provided for a Serb-controlled republic and a Bosniak-Muslim federation within a nationwide federation of Bosnia-Herzegovina.

The task of rebuilding the country began soon after, although this would take years even with foreign help. No accurate account of those killed can be made, and the UN estimates that 2 million people were displaced as entire towns and villages were destroyed. One intangible that cannot easily be restored is the trust between the different religious groups.

WAR CRIME TRIALS

In 1993 the UN International Criminal Tribunal began investigating accusations of war crimes committed by Bosnian Serbs and Yugoslav Serbs in their policy of ethnic cleansing. It took time to identify those involved and then to have them arrested or to persuade them to give themselves up. The tribunal, meeting at The Hague in the Netherlands, also decided that rape was a war crime; it had been used as a "weapon" by the Serbs because they knew that in Bosnian Muslim culture, the rape victim could never be accepted back into her family or community.

By 1999 several key figures had been indicted, including the commander of one of the concentration camps and his officers. Major General Radislav Krstic was the highest ranking officer to be put on trial, and on August 2, 2001, he was found guilty in the mass killing of more than 7,000 Muslim men, women, and children at Srebrenica in 1995. The president of Serbia (Yugoslavia), Slobodan Milosevic *(below)*, was also indicted for his role in ordering the genocide.

The Tribunal's work ground on slowly through the early years of the new century. By 2003 dozens of lesser officials and camp guards had been found guilty; they received sentences ranging from 12 to 30 years. Although more than 100 people were indicted, more than 5,000 others have been accused. The tribunal hopes to complete its work by 2006, so UN officials plan to speed the process by establishing a local tribunal in Bosnia.

GOVERNMENT

FOR HALF A CENTURY AFTER World War II, Bosnia-Herzegovina was one of the six republics making up the Yugoslav Federation. The Communist Party under Marshal Tito controlled both the government and the economy. After Tito's death in 1980, the Communists' hold steadily weakened as the economy declined, and in 1990, Bosnia held its first democratic, multiparty elections. The Communists then relinquished control to a coalition of three parties: the Party of Democratic Action (SDA), which represented most Bosnian Muslims, the Serb Democratic Party (SDP), and the Croat Democratic Union of Bosnia-Herzegovina (HDZ).

The new government, like the three parties, was designed to represent the country's major ethnic groups. Provision was also made for a three-person revolving presidency consisting of a Bosniak, a Serb, and a Croat. In 1992, however, Bosnia-Herzegovina declared its independence from Yugoslavia, despite opposition from Bosnian Serbs, who wanted to remain a part of Yugoslavia.

Soon after, the Serbs pulled out of the new government; the Croats did the same, with the argument that they did not want to remain in a country that would be dominated by Muslims. This turned the conflict into a three-way war. The Bosnian Muslims, now attacked by both Croats and Serbs, still managed to raise an army and defend the roughly one-third of the state still in their control, including the besieged capital of Sarajevo. In 1994 the Croats and Bosniaks agreed to a cease-fire, and the Croats joined the struggle against the Serbs.

Above: **Bosnians age 18 and above may vote.**

Opposite: **The Stabilization Force (SFOR) of about 30,000 troops replaced the NATO Implementation Force in 1996. SFOR troops were reduced to 18,000 in 2001.**

33

INTERNATIONAL INTERVENTION

The international community became deeply involved in the plight of Bosnia-Herzegovina through the Dayton (Ohio) Agreement, signed in late 1995. The UN supported sending in a NATO force to enforce the Dayton provisions. This Implementation Force (IFOR) was changed to the Stabilization Force (SFOR) in 1996, after the fighting stopped. SFOR was made up of soldiers from 18 NATO nations, including the United States, and 16 non-NATO countries.

Another agency—the Organization for Security and Cooperation in Europe (OSCE)—was sent in to supervise elections and to maintain a balance among ethnic groups.

Seated, from left to right: **President Zubak of the Federation of Bosnia and Herzegovina and President Izetbegovic of the Republic of Bosnia and Herzegovina sign the Dayton Agreement in Paris, France in 1995.**

Men in Tuzla unpack sacks of food supplies sent by the United States to aid Bosnians in the civil war.

Other international agencies have also been involved in governing the war-damaged country. The Office of the High Representative for Bosnia-Herzegovina oversees the implementation of the Dayton Agreement and also examines any reports of human rights violations. The UN provided an International Police Task Force to train new police forces and to help identify and arrest those suspected of committing war crimes. In addition, the UN, the United States, and the European Union have sent money, supplies, and aid workers to assist the war's victims, including more than 2 million refugees.

THE NATIONAL GOVERNMENT

The Dayton Agreement established Bosnia's current government, following the original 1990 structure. The country is divided into two semi-independent entities: the Republika Srpska (Serb Republic), which controls about 49 percent of the territory; and the Bosniak-Croat Federacija (Bosniak-Croat Federation), which has 51 percent.

DIVISION OF RESPONSIBILITY Both the Republic and the Federation govern their own affairs, but matters concerning the entire country are the responsibility of a third entity—the Bosne I Hercegovine Federacija (Bosnia-Herzegovina Federation). While the Serb Republic and the Bosniak-Croat Federation each has a parliament and president, the state again has a joint presidency divided along ethnic lines. It includes one Serb, chosen from the Republic, plus one Bosniak and one Croat, chosen from the Federation.

The national parliament consists of two houses: the House of Representatives and the House of Peoples. The House of Representatives has 42 members, 28 from the Federation and 14 from the Republic. The House of Peoples has 15 members chosen by the local parliaments and must include five Bosniaks, five Croats, and five Serbs.

The day-to-day administration of the country is in the hands of the Council of Ministers. Each minister heads an administrative department, such as transportation, finance, foreign policy, and trade.

THE MINE ACTION CENTER

One of the grimmest legacies of the war is the continued presence of land mines *(below)* placed in conflict zones by the warring parties between 1992 and 1995. Overseeing the task of discovering and defusing the deadly mines is another UN agency—the Mine Action Centre (MAC)—with headquarters in Sarajevo. The center coordinates activities of the NATO troops, the various police agencies, and its own small staff. MAC staff estimate that, as of 2003, more than one million mines still have to be found and detonated; they say that only about 60 percent of the minefields have been reported. They estimate that it would take "1,000 mine clearers 38 years to clear all areas." A related problem is that of unexploded ordnance (UXO), consisting of mortars, artillery shells, and grenades, which are still immensely dangerous.

THE SEARCH FOR A STABLE GOVERNMENT

The ethnic and religious divisions in Bosnia-Herzegovina made it nearly impossible to form an effective government. For a time during the civil war, each group formed its own government. The Croat and Serb governments simply ignored the decisions of the Muslim-dominated legal government.

From 1995 to 1998, the only effective nationwide government was provided by Carlos Westendorp, the High Representative. The position was established by the European Union and the U.S. government to oversee the carrying out of the Dayton accord. When the legislature

Spanish diplomat Carlos Westendorp *(left)*, **the international community's High Representative to Bosnia, welcomes Canadian Defence Minister Art Eggleton** *(right)* **in his office in Sarajevo in 1998. The Canadian minister was on a one-day official visit to Sarajevo.**

could not reach a decision on any issue, Westendorp simply ruled by proclamation.

In the 1998 elections Westendorp even removed some officeholders and disqualified several candidates because he was convinced they did not support the Dayton accord. He even chose the new flag for Bosnia when the president and legislature could not agree. The major concern about the flag was to make sure that none of the flag's elements would have political meaning to any of the country's factions.

THE NATIONAL ANTHEM

The music to the national anthem is based on an old folk song *S one strane Plive'* (*On the Other Side of the River Pliva*). In 1995 the government held a contest for lyrics to the anthem. Sarajevan pop singer Dino Merlin won the honor.

I pledge my loyalty to you
My thousand-year-old land
From Sava to the sea
From Drina to Una

You are unique
My only homeland
You are unique
Bosnia and Herzegovina

May God save you
For the generations to come
You are my land of dreams
The land of my forefathers

ECONOMY

THE 43 MONTHS OF CIVIL WAR in the 1990s had a devastating impact on the economy, as it did on all aspects of Bosnian life. In the early years of the 21st century, the people still struggle to overcome the massive postwar problems of refugees, homelessness, and unemployment that remains above 30 percent of the workforce. In spite of the scope of the problems, Bosnians are making outstanding progress in rebuilding the country and creating a modern economy.

Even before the war Bosnia's experience with 45 years of Communism left the country with huge economic difficulties. The Communist regime established by Tito in the late 1940s remained independent of the Soviet Union but suffered from many of the same weaknesses as the Soviet system. The theory of communism, as developed by Karl Marx, was that the state, or government, would manage the economy for a time and then the state mechanism would "wither away." The trouble was that the state never began to wither away. Instead, it became an enormous, entrenched bureaucracy, bound in red tape, and self-perpetuating.

In Yugoslavia, including Bosnia-Herzegovina, the factories, mines, and distribution businesses were run by workers' councils, with the workers electing representatives to operate each business. The state, in turn, established planning boards, which set production goals for every part of the economy. To win awards for meeting goals and avoid punishment for falling short, managers in every factory, shop, and mining operation quickly learned to accept shoddy raw materials simply to keep production going. Regional inspectors passed over inferior products because the quantity of goods was what counted to the bureaucracy, not quality.

Above: **People stroll by shops selling metal and fabric goods in Sarajevo. Though trade within the country is improving, Bosnia-Herzegovina is still in a poor trade position internationally.**

Opposite: **Timber is an important contributor to the economy and is an export commodity.**

41

Timber is brought to factories like this one, which produces furniture. Apart from the wooden furniture industry, Bosnia's manufacturing sector also consists of minerals, textiles, oil refinery, and vehicle assembly.

ENVIRONMENTAL EFFECTS The emphasis on building a great industrial economy by extracting more and more natural resources and building more factories was disastrous for the environment. State bureaucrats paid little attention to the shocking increase in the pollution of air, water, and land. Cleanup operations, begun in the late 1990s, will continue well into the 21st century.

Even with the Communist legacy of inefficiency and environmental disaster, Bosnia- Herzegovina has the building blocks for a healthy mixed economy. Agriculture, logging, mining, manufacturing, and services are all important contributors to the economy.

AGRICULTURE AND FORESTRY

The northern two-thirds of Bosnia-Herzegovina has good farmland, especially in the fertile river valleys. Grains are the major crops—wheat and corn, and also fodder crops for cattle, sheep, and pigs. A wide variety of table vegetables are grown, and the eastern part of the country is famous for its fruits, particularly plums and figs. Farm families also grow a number of specialized crops, including sugar beets, hemp, sunflowers, and grapes for wine. Through much of the year, open-air markets and bazaars display a colorful array of fruits, vegetables, meats, fish, and cut flowers.

Timber has long been an important component of the economy, and roughly one-third of the land is forested. Pine and fir are harvested for board lumber and plywood, while hardwoods, such as walnut and oak, are used for furniture manufacturing.

MINING AND MANUFACTURING

Although the country is not rich in minerals, there are adequate supplies, and there is extensive mining of coal, iron, copper, salt, and zinc. These resources, plus oil refining, form the basis for Bosnia's manufacturing of steel, textiles, furniture, and building materials. The textile industry produces rugs, carpets, wall hangings, and other decorative items of outstanding quality, both handmade and factory-produced.

During the civil war industrial production was cut by more than 75 percent and more than half the labor force were thrown out of work. Rebuilding, with help from the international community and the United States, was slow because of the need to restore the infrastructure —roads, bridges, electric power lines, transportation systems, and communication networks—as well as to rebuild buildings and to replace machinery. By 2003 output was inching back up to prewar levels, but unemployment remained high.

Grapes and wines are produced in the eastern part of the country, where the climate is favorable.

Above: **A stall at Kujund Ziluk Street in Mostar sells beautiful rugs and carpets.**

Opposite: **Tourists cross the Stari Most bridge. The service industry contributes to 46 percent of the country's gross domestic product (GDP).**

FINANCE AND TRADE

Bosnia-Herzegovina is in a poor trade position, partly because of war. Even with massive amounts of international aid, the country needs to import nearly $3 billion worth of goods every year, while exporting only $450 million worth of its products. This kind of imbalance is a drain on the nation's limited money supply. Bosnia's GDP—the total of its production of materials, products, and services—is $7.3 billion per year, which is an average of $1,900 per person, one of the lowest per capita figures in Europe. (By contrast, the per capita output in neighboring Croatia is $5100.)

Since 1998 Bosnia's monetary unit has been the convertible marka, with 1.57 markas equal to one U.S. dollar. (Convertible means that the markas can be exchanged for other currencies.) Travel agents say that the monetary exchange rates should encourage travelers, but income from tourism remains a miniscule $37 million per year (2001), another legacy of the war. As the country continues to stabilize, there are indications that tourism will increase at a much healthier rate.

MODERNIZATION AND SERVICES

The greatest change in the Bosnian economy since the war has been in its connection to the outside world. Beginning with the arrival of thousands of NATO troops from more than 30 countries, plus several thousand people from various international agencies, Bosnians have become increasingly aware of different styles, tastes, and technologies.

People now routinely buy CDs featuring eastern European and U.S. bands and vocalists.

Through television, films, radio, and, above all, the Internet, Bosnians are up-to-date on clothing styles, fads, and media favorites. Kids are eager to have the latest video games, T-shirts, posters, and other trappings of the global youth culture.

Along with the modernization of Bosnian life, there has been a great increase in service industries, such as education, banking, government, restaurants, hotels, and transportation. In addition, the war led to a huge increase in health services, including help for those disabled by war injuries and counseling for trauma victims, many of them refugee children. By 1999 services amounted to 60 percent of the nation's economy.

ENVIRONMENT

PERMANENT SETTLEMENTS have existed in the Balkan region of southeastern Europe for 4,000 years or more. The continued use of the land for farms and villages has steadily altered the environment and, over time, created stresses on natural systems. Even industry has a far longer history in the region than in more recently developed nations such as the United States. The burning of coal, for example, and the smelting of iron have been common in Bosnia for well over a thousand years.

For centuries, human-engineered changes led to only localized environmental damage, such as erosion caused by logging a steep hillside. In fact, the damage was quite insignificant until the Communists came to power. As soon as Marshal Tito and the Communists assumed power after World War II, they became single-minded in their drive to turn what was then Yugoslavia into an industrialized and urbanized state. No one paid attention to the impact on the environment. During the 45 years of Communist rule following World War II, more damage was done to the environment in the region than in all the previous centuries of human activity combined.

The destruction that resulted from the civil war added to the environmental chaos, and the years of war prevented the government from trying to resolve some of the worst problems. In the early years of the 21st century, the new government and the people of Bosnia-Herzegovina are working feverishly to restore the nation's environmental health. The agencies of the UN and other international agencies are helping in a variety of ways.

Above: **A sign marking the entrance to Tuzla, a town in the northeastern part of Bosnia-Herzegovina, stands near a coal-burning electrical plant. Approximately 54 percent of the country's electricity is supplied by fossil fuel.**

Opposite: **Goats stand on a rocky perch. The government is working on expanding the area of wildlife sanctuaries and forest reserves.**

Marshal Tito (right) waves from a window of his train shortly before leaving for Moscow on an official visit in June 1956. Standing next to him are his wife, and Edvard Kardelj, vice president of the Federal Executive Council. Marshal Tito was among the people responsible for steering Yugoslavia toward industrialization.

THE LEGACY OF COMMUNISM

The Communists used outdated coal-burning furnaces and antiquated machinery because that was what was immediately available. As the number of factories multiplied, the smog hanging over the cities steadily thickened. Rivers and lakes began to look eerily unhealthy. Water supplies began to taste strange, and there were no government regulations limiting what factories, mines, and communities could dump into rivers and lakes.

Like government leaders in other Communist countries, Yugoslav officials insisted that these were minor problems and constituted the price that had to be paid to catch up with the capitalist countries of western Europe and North America. The officials refused to release figures on pollutants from power plants, or to reveal what pollutants were being spewed into the air by the new steel mills and manufacturing establishments. Tito's government controlled the media, so the people learned little about the environmental alarms being raised by international environmental groups. Foreign reporters were denied access to Yugoslav facilities.

In spite of official efforts to ignore the problems, evidence suggesting that all of eastern Europe was facing ecocatastrophe began to leak out. In neighboring Romania, for example, photographs from the town of Copsa Mica showed that everything in the community of 7,000 was covered with a thick layer of carbon black, a pollutant from tire manufacturing; people could not get their clothing or their skin free of the soot, and even the sheep were black. A report from a steel mill in southern Poland indicating that 80 percent of the workers retired with disabilities suggested the dangers posed by the outmoded facilities throughout the region.

The end of nearly all the Communist regimes in eastern Europe during 1989–90, including Yugoslavia, allowed the new non-Communist governments to begin assessing the environmental fallout from the 45-year experiment with Communism. In Bosnia-Herzegovina, the first efforts were interrupted by the civil war. But as soon as the fighting stopped, Bosnians went back to work energetically, even sending a delegation to the World Conservation Congress in Montreal in 1996.

A woman checks radiation levels after the Chernobyl nuclear explosion in the Soviet Union. The 1986 explosion, the worst nuclear disaster in history, heightened all Eastern Europeans' awareness of their vulnerability in such incidents.

A street in Bosnia is crowded with truckloads of refugees on their way to refugee camps.

AIR POLLUTION

In addressing their ecological disaster, Bosnians found that every aspect of their industries was contributing to the dangerous levels of pollution. Cause-and-effect relationships were sometimes difficult to identify. The smelting of iron ore, for example, produces cadmium and lead—two deadly carcinogens; dust containing these elements at one mill was falling on nearby vegetable gardens kept by the steelworkers' families, thus entering the food chain and contributing to high levels of lung and kidney disease.

Even when the cause was clear, the solutions were likely to be complicated, or costly, or both. For instance, coal-burning power plants produce great amounts of sulfur dioxide, but purchasing and installing the scrubbers (devices that trap particles from gaseous emissions to prevent them from entering the atmosphere) and other antipollution devices take time, special skills, and perhaps more money than most electric companies can afford. Those power plants, plus pollution from smelting plants and motor vehicle emissions, are the worst producers of acid rain. In Bosnia-Herzegovina, acid rain—precipitation that drops high levels of sulfuric and nitric acids—has destroyed coniferous forests at low elevations and is thought to be a major contributor to the pollution of some lakes and ponds. So far, efforts to provide catalytic converters for motor vehicles, and other technological solutions, are being pursued cautiously because of the cost and the need for technological expertise.

WATER POLLUTION

One of the major sources of Bosnia's water pollution woes is agriculture. The modernization and mechanization of farming, especially in the 20th century, has led to a tremendous increase in food production, but the cost has been great. The development of large single-crop fields and the increased use of irrigation have required the heavy use of chemical fertilizers and pesticides. These chemicals enter the food chain and also leach into the groundwater, eventually reaching the nearest body of water. Pollutants, such as nitrates and phosphates, cause a buildup of algae in lakes and ponds. That buildup, in turn, leads to a loss of nutrients, killing the algae; the decomposing algae lower oxygen levels, resulting in the death of fish and other marine life.

Government investigators have found that factories routinely dump heavy metals, chemicals, and untreated sewage into the nation's waterways. Court action to force the offenders to stop or to pay fines has been a slow and cumbersome process.

The inadequate, and sometimes nonexistent, sewage treatment facilities in Bosnia contribute to water pollution. This, in turn, causes problems with drinking water.

This hydroelectric power plant is built on a river near Zvornik in the eastern part of the country. The U.S. Agency for International Development (USAID) helped install equipment at another power plant in Kakanj, making it one of the cleanest plants in Europe. It restored power to local industries and to more than 750,000 residents of the region.

INTERNATIONAL COOPERATION

While other former-Communist countries were struggling to end state-controlled economies and clean up the environmental mess, Bosnia-Herzegovina was held back by the civil war and the damage it caused. In fact, NATO bombing of Serb-held areas destroyed factories and oil refineries, releasing more pollutants into the air and water. By the year 2000, however, international cooperation helped the environmental movement to start gaining momentum.

One area in which international aid has helped has been in finding out the scope of the problem and the source of the worst pollution. For example, the Japan Special Fund set up a research project that identified hundreds of illegal dumping sites throughout the Balkans, including Bosnia. This information enabled the Serb Republic and the Bosniak-Croat Federation to crack down on the violators.

Another step toward restoring environmental health has involved educating government and business leaders on what can be done and what new technologies are available. The UN Environment Programme has established facilities for training legislators and other government officials. Similarly, the Organization for Security and Cooperation in Europe (OSCE) shows each country's decision makers how to make better use of resources without causing ecological damage.

Financial aid has also been important to Bosnia's efforts. The European Union donated $60 million in the year 2000 to help establish environmentally safer production methods, while USAID helped to restore water supplies and electrical service to roughly half the population by 2002.

PROTECTING THE LAND

In the late 1990s a UN survey revealed that Bosnia-Herzegovina had less than 1 percent of its land set aside as wildlife sanctuaries or forest reserves, the lowest figure for any country in Europe. Even struggling countries like Slovakia had more than 10 percent of their land preserved. The pollution of some waterways has led to a decline in marine life, and this in turn reduces the number of birds. The government is in the process of identifying forest and wildlife areas that can be set aside as protected. The World Wildlife Federation and other international organizations are providing technical assistance. Experts say that Bosnia is fortunate to have so many mountain rivers, lakes, and forest regions that have not suffered severe environmental damage. These resources will provide a solid basis for creating parks and reserves.

Less than 1 percent of the land in Bosnia is set aside as forest reserves, while acid rain has destroyed some coniferous forests.

BOSNIANS

UNTIL BOSNIA-HERZEGOVINA exploded in civil war in 1992, the country had survived with sharp ethnic divisions. From the 15th century on, the three main ethnic-religious groups lived side by side more or less peacefully, often sharing the same town or city neighborhood.

The three groups—Bosnian Muslims (Bosniaks), Croats, and Serbs—actually belong to the same racial, or ethnic, group. All are descendants of the South Slavs who migrated into the region in the fifth and sixth centuries A.D. The differences among the groups would seem to be based more on religion than on ethnic background. Most Croats are Roman Catholics; Bosnian Serbs belong to the Eastern Orthodox Church; and Bosniaks are followers of Islam. In almost any city, it is not unusual to see the spire of a Catholic church alongside the bell tower of an Orthodox church and the minaret of an Islamic mosque.

In the 20th century, however, the powerful force of nationalism began to create deeper divisions. In 1912 and 1913, two separate Balkan Wars erupted as several groups battled to establish independent nations out of the crumbling Ottoman Empire. Bulgaria, Serbia, Montenegro, and Macedonia were involved in these struggles against the Ottomans after Montenegro declared war against Turkey on October 8, 1912. The countries fought against each other in 1913 over the division of Macedonia among the victors. In the 1980s and 1990s nationalism surfaced again as Communist Yugoslavia began to break apart. It was during these years that nationalism came to be associated with religion.

Above: **Wounded soldiers from the Balkan Wars lie under blankets in an ambulance tent.**

Opposite: **Almost 19 percent of people in the country are 14 years of age and below.**

Bosnian Muslims pray behind coffins during a mass funeral for people who were killed during the Serbs' ethnic cleansing drive. The remains of these Muslims were found in different mass graves a few years after the civil war ended.

ETHNIC CLEANSING

Bosnian Serbs wanted a strong, independent Serbia. To them, that meant getting rid of the two non-Serb groups—Muslim Bosniaks and Catholic Croats. The Croats, in turn, hoped to be part of an expanded, independent Croatia. The Bosnian Muslims were seen as a stumbling block to the nationalistic aspirations of both groups.

Religious differences that had been tolerated for so long were now seen as symbols of the "enemy"—a source of fear and hatred. When the fighting began, Serb troops not only attacked Muslim people but also ruthlessly destroyed mosques, bazaars, and other buildings associated with Islam.

The people of Bosnia-Herzegovina had first experienced ethnic cleansing, or genocide, during World War II, when Croatian Nazis, the Ustasa, dragged thousands of Serbs, Jews, and Roma (Gypsies) from their homes. Many were taken to remote forests and executed; others were shipped to Nazi death camps.

During the Bosnian civil war (1992–95), Bosnian Serbs, with help from the largely Serb Yugoslav army, made a determined bid to destroy or drive out the country's Muslim population. NATO forces first tried to stop the mass killings by establishing a series of safe zones, where Muslim refugees could escape the Serb death squads.

In July 1995, however, the Serbs attacked the safe area of Srebrenica, which is a town in the eastern part of Bosnia-Herzegovina, and butchered more than 7,000 Bosniaks as they tried to flee into a forest. These atrocities led NATO to step up its military intervention and the UN War Crimes Tribunal to take more vigorous action.

DESTROYING TOLERANCE

The war bred hatred and left a legacy of bitterness. It was also costly in terms of the numbers killed—an estimated 7.4 percent of the prewar Muslim population and about 7.1 percent of the Serbian population; Croat casualties were somewhat lower.

RELIGIOUS ATTACKS For the first two years of the war, Bosnia's Muslims were under attack from both Serb forces and Croats. Between 1992 and 1994, well-equipped Croat troops attacked a number of towns that had large numbers of Bosniaks. Mostar, the country's second largest city, was besieged much the way Sarajevo was, only in this case by Croats. The Croats hoped to make the city their capital, but their artillery destroyed the Catholic church, a 19th-century Orthodox church, and scores of Islamic mosques. More than 2,000 people were killed during this siege, thousands fled, and more than 5,000 buildings were destroyed.

Mostar is coming back to life in the postwar years. But the tolerance and acceptance of the past have disappeared. Croats remain on the western side of the Neretva River and Bosniaks on the eastern side, except for a narrow strip on the Croat side. The people of each group tend to regard the other with caution, sometimes with suspicion or fear.

Two men return to their village to rebuild their home, which was damaged in the war. Financial aid from the United States and other countries is helping to restore homes and apartments in Bosnia-Herzegovina. In Mostar, shops, restaurants, and nightclubs are back in business.

THE BRIDGE AT MOSTAR—A NEW SYMBOL

A magnificent bridge with a gleaming white arch spanned the Neretva River at Mostar. The bridge, called Stari Most—Turkish for old bridge—was built by the Ottoman Turks in the 16th century. According to legend, the arch covered such a large span that the great Turkish ruler, Suleyman the Magnificent, ordered that the builder, architect Mimar Hajrudin, be executed if the arch collapsed. Hajrudin fled just before the scaffolding was removed. He could have remained. The bridge, between two jagged bluffs, remained solid for four centuries.

Over many generations Stari Most became a symbol of unity between the Muslims on the eastern side of the bridge and the Croats on the western side. It was also known for the displays of high diving by daredevils who plunged 65 feet (20 m) into the churning waters of the Neretva.

When the civil war began, the bridge was badly damaged by artillery fire. But then in November 1993, Bosnian Croats provoked outrage by shelling the damaged arch again and again, until it crashed into the river *(above)*.

The project of rebuilding the bridge became a new symbol—a symbol of the effort to reconcile a community and nation that was now bitterly divided. As early as 1996, Austria provided funds and Turkey sent engineers skilled in building with limestone. In August 2003 the Muslim mayor of Mostar and his deputy, a Croat, helped use a crane to lift a gigantic keystone into place in the middle of the 86-foot (27-m) span. Mustafa Selimovic, a retired Muslim professor, said, "This bridge has to bring people together, because bridges are about peace and people living side by side."

Above: **A Jewish woman touches a name at a memorial in Sarajevo that was erected in honor of the Jews killed in World War II.**

Opposite: **A Roma woman sells electrical goods and chinaware at a market.**

TWO SPECIAL MINORITIES

Two small minorities continue to exist in Bosnia-Herzegovina in spite of heavy persecution.

JEWS Jews migrated into the Balkan region at several different times, the first as early as the fifth century A.D. This first migration was a result of differences between Jews and Christians. Jews had rejected Christianity and Christians, as a result, had regarded Jews as a foreign people. Perhaps the largest numbers came during the Spanish Inquisition in 1492, when 160,000 Jews were expelled from Spain after King Ferdinand and Queen Isabella I issued an edict against them in March that year. Other Jews came in the 19th and 20th centuries to escape persecution in Poland and Russia. While forced to live in separate ghettos in most of Europe, Jews found a more friendly reception in Muslim areas. Most Bosnian Jews have been city dwellers, and a large percentage have been professionals, including teachers and physicians. They added important dimensions to the culture of Bosnia-Herzegovina.

From 1933 to 1945, during Adolph Hitler's vicious campaign to destroy the Jews of Europe, an estimated 6 million Jews were killed in Nazi concentration camps scattered throughout eastern and southern Europe. A few thousand returned to cities like Sarajevo and Mostar, but the numbers have remained small. There is a Jewish museum in Sarajevo and a synagogue, but in most of Bosnia, empty synagogues and untended cemeteries are stark reminders of the once vibrant Jewish culture.

ROMA The people known as Gypsies once numbered up to 4 million throughout Europe. They had originally migrated west from northern India in the 11th century A.D. They have always been fiercely independent, living a nomadic life and wandering throughout Europe with little regard for national borders. They are known today as Roma. Their language, Romany, is not a written language but has been used by Roma throughout the world. The Romany language, unknown to others, has been useful to Roma as a kind of secret code, but it has also served to make authorities suspicious of them. The world's largest Roma populations have been in eastern Europe and as many as 100,000 lived in scattered tribes in the hills and mountains of Bosnia-Herzegovina before World War II. Like Jews, they were victims of Hitler's policy of genocide and several million died in the death camps.

The Roma have traditionally held occupations on the fringes of society—junk dealers, horse traders, circus performers, and fortune-tellers. Their colorful way of life has appealed to novelists and filmmakers, and their music has had a lasting influence, providing melodies for contemporary songwriters and for classical composers such as Franz Liszt. Fewer than 20,000 remain in Bosnia today.

LIFESTYLE

LIFE IN BOSNIA-HERZEGOVINA is in a state of transition—the transition from a government-controlled, Communist society to a capitalistic, free market nation. For people living in the Soviet bloc countries, this massive change began with the collapse of Communism in 1989–90. The end of Communist control was a signal to start living—to embrace and enjoy the materialistic lifestyle of western Europe and North America.

Above: **Years after the civil war, families in Sarajevo still live in war-damaged houses.**

Opposite: **Bosnians walk to work on a street in Sarajevo. The ratio of men to women in the country is almost equal.**

Bosnians began the same rush to freedom only to have it stalled by the civil war (1992–95). The cost of the war was enormous: thousands were killed, thousands more maimed for life; cities like Sarajevo and Mostar were heavily damaged; entire towns and villages were destroyed; and nearly 2 million people were homeless refugees. The economy was at a standstill, with roughly half the workforce unemployed.

The war led to far-reaching changes in people's way of living. Villages and urban neighborhoods are no longer rainbows of different ethnic-religious groups. People from different religious groups have lost the trust they once had in one another. Muslim families now prefer to live near other Muslims. The same is true of Croats and Serbs, although people in those two groups tend to be more tolerant of each other than of Muslims. Political leaders increase the division by supporting cultural projects that lead each group to regard itself as inherently different from the others.

Within each group, family ties remain central to the way people live. The family home has always been of great importance, so the destruction of entire villages has been devastating. Health-care workers say that post-traumatic stress counseling has been vital in helping children and adults restore a sense of family and home after years in refugee camps and often the loss of one or more family members.

People enjoy the atmosphere at an outdoor café. In the background is the Gazi Husref-Bey Mosque, which was built in the 16th century and named after a Bosnian governor who ruled during the time.

LIFE IN SARAJEVO

Sarajevo, the capital of Bosnia-Herzegovina, was long regarded as the jewel of the Balkans. Even the setting is spectacular, with the city hugging the narrow valley of the Miljacka River and Mount Trebevic providing a picturesque backdrop.

Sarajevo was—and still is—the most Asian-influenced city in Europe, having been built in the 15th and 16th centuries by the Ottoman Turks as their provincial capital. The name came from the Turkish *saraj ovasi*, meaning the land around the governor's palace. During the 16th century, Sarajevo's golden age, the Ottoman Turks built 70 mosques, symbols of their success in converting people to Islam. Even today, the magnificent clock tower and the partially restored mosques and minarets are visual reminders of the city's Turkish heritage.

Suburbs were built on the hillsides surrounding the city, which generally lack the outstanding architecture. Even the entire village built for the 1984 Winter Olympics seems ordinary compared with Sarajevo itself.

During the civil war Bosnian Serbs laid siege to the city for three years and the shelling reduced hundreds of buildings to rubble. The only route to the outside world was a mile-long (1.6 km) tunnel beneath the airport. (Part of the tunnel has now been reopened as a war museum.) The city's main boulevard became known as Sniper's Alley, where hundreds of Sarajevans were killed or wounded by high-powered snipers' rifles as they attempted to cross the open space.

TUNNEL OF HOPE

In 1993 Sarajevans began building a tunnel between the airport and the adjacent suburbs. The airport was a neutral zone controlled by the UN. The 875-yard (800 m) tunnel was dug by volunteers using picks, shovels, and wheelbarrows. Supplies—food, oil, medication—as well as the injured were transported in and out of the city through the tunnel. Without it the city might have fallen. The remains of the tunnel—66 feet (20 m)—are preserved as a museum.

Schoolmates of 11-year-old Bosnian girl Ema Alic cry during her funeral at a cemetery in Sarajevo. Ema and two other young Sarajevans were killed in a mine blast on the slopes of Mount Trebevic. The mountain overlooks the Bosnian capital, near the former frontline of the civil war. Thousands of land-mines still lie hidden in the ground around Sarajevo, which was besieged by Bosnian Serb forces during the conflict.

Alleys in the Turkish Quarter are lined with shops that display brightly colored carpets and wall hangings, jewelry, or household items crafted in bronze or copper.

POST-WAR SARAJEVO Today, less than a decade after the war, Sarajevo is again a lively city, bursting with renewed energy. Shops and restaurants reopened even as battered buildings were being repaired. Brightly colored trams (streetcars) now clang along Sniper's Alley, and in the evening people again stroll along Ferhadija, the main pedestrian thoroughfare, or sip Turkish coffee at one of the many outdoor cafés. Foreign visitors have begun to return, too, including thousands who are connected to the many international agencies that have offices in the city. These visitors come from more than 30 countries, giving Sarajevo a cosmopolitan feel.

The section of the city that represents Sarajevo's uniqueness is the Turkish quarter—Bascarsija. Here the cobblestone streets and alleys are lined with Middle Eastern-style shops. There are still a few wooden houses with ornate interiors dating from the time in the 16th century when Sarajevo was the only European city with public baths and free meals for the poor. The city also has modern businesses, including a furniture factory, a brewery, and a sugar-beet refinery.

STARTING OVER

The story of Dr. Sima Suler demonstrates how the years of civil war have affected people's way of life long after the fighting stopped.

Dr. Suler was just beginning her medical career and her family life when the war erupted in 1992. She was a Bosniak, and her husband, known as Duke, was of mixed parentage—a Croatian mother and a Serb father. But like most Bosnians, the young couple was not troubled by the ethnic mixing. When the Bosnian Serbs and units of the Yugoslav army surrounded the city, however, the couple became concerned by the ethnic or religious animosity that emerged. Then when their first child was born with a serious ailment, they decided that Sima would have to try to get out of Sarajevo and seek medical help through friends in the United States.

"The next 10 years were so hard," Dr. Suler recalled in a 2003 interview with the *Pittsburgh Post Gazette*. "My brother was killed and my husband was trapped in Sarajevo." She was able to escape Sarajevo with UN peacekeepers forming a shield to help her across Sniper's Alley *(below)* and then escorting her through the escape tunnel. Once in the United States, the infant received the medical care he needed and she was able to complete her medical training.

When the siege of Sarajevo was lifted, the Sulers' troubles were still not over. Since Duke was a Serb, he was expected to fight in the Serbian army in a secondary war against the Yugoslav province of Kosovo, a conflict that continued into the late 1990s. But Duke refused to fight and was put in a Serb prison.

Now, a full 10 years after the fighting began, the family is reunited, and Dr. Suler is about to begin her long-delayed medical practice. "I'm 40 years old," she says, "and I feel like I'm just starting my life over again." Many Bosnians feel the same way.

After the civil war ended, people resumed their daily activities. Elderly men in Banja Luka once again sit in parks or at sidewalk cafés playing chess, talking, some drinking thick black coffee, others sipping a local drink called *nektar*.

LIFE IN BANJA LUKA

Banja Luka, a city of about 230,000 on the banks of the Vrbas River, is the capital of the Serb Republic (Republika Srpska). Originally established by the Illyrians around 300 B.C., and later a Roman town, it has seen its share of upheaval. In the 19th century it was the center of Bosnian revolts against the Turks. During World War II (1939–45), it was occupied by the Ustasa—the Croatian fascists— who displayed their anti-Muslim sentiments by damaging, and sometimes destroying, some 70 mosques and minarets, including a great domed mosque called Ferhad Pasha, built during the Ottoman rule in 1583. In the midst of rebuilding after the war, widespread damage occurred again due to an earthquake in 1969. Then, during the 1992–95 civil war the Bosnian Serbs took a turn by blowing up 16 mosques, the only damage the city suffered during that conflict.

Now, in the aftermath of the civil war, the people of Banja Luka are trying to return to a more normal way of life. Women again hang out their laundry and exchange gossip about TV soap opera stars or local scandals.

While life seems normal on the surface, there is the sense that something is missing—a feeling that a certain kind of energy or vitality has not come back. It may be that that energy was a product of diversity—of the different groups living and working together in Banja Luka—but locals deny this. The fact is, however, that before the war, Banja Luka was quite evenly divided along ethnic-religious lines, roughly half Serb and a little less than half Muslim. Today, the population is almost 100 percent Serb.

GENDER ROLES

Until the 1950s the roles performed by men and women were clearly defined, with men as the breadwinners and women caring for the home and family. An easing of this strict separation began under the Communists, when the government pursued an official policy of equality. Some women joined the Communist party and began to pry open doors of opportunity for women, including careers in professions such as medicine, law, and engineering. For most families, however, especially in rural areas, traditional roles remained unchanged.

Greater steps toward equality have been taken since 1990, as women have pressed for greater opportunities in education and jobs. Women began to adopt Western clothing styles, and the number of women working outside the home has grown steadily.

A Muslim Bosnian woman works as a cashier in a shop. Communism helped change the traditional notion that husbands were the sole breadwinners.

This drive for greater equality between the sexes has not been as important to Muslim women. Because their religion and culture have been under attack, many Muslim women have become more conservative, perhaps as a way of displaying pride in their heritage. Rural women have always been more conservative in clothing styles, wearing longer skirts or loose-fitting pants, and a growing number have returned to wearing the chador—a head scarf that can be raised to cover the lower part of the face. In general, however, Bosniak women are not subject to the same constraints as Muslim women in other countries. In fact, in Sarajevo and Mostar, Muslim women often cannot be distinguished from Croat or Serbian women, since they wear Western-style clothing and work in offices, shops, and restaurants.

A girl and her grandmother, dressed in traditional farm clothes, stop for a break in the fields.

COUNTRY AND CITY

Slightly more than half of Bosnia's population lives in rural areas—mostly small farm villages. As in other societies, rural Bosnians tend to be a little distrustful of outsiders and uneasy about new ideas or ways of doing things. Their farming methods often seem more appropriate to the early 1900s than to the early 2000s. Tastes in everything from clothing styles to music tend to favor tradition.

In spite of their distrust, rural Bosnians are considered warm and friendly, with a strong sense of being hospitable. A favorite time of day is the coffee hour, a time to visit with friends and neighbors. Women will gather in a neighbor's kitchen or dooryard with cups of coffee and their embroidery. While they talk, they stitch colorful designs on scarves, towels, blouses, and other items.

There is a strong oral tradition in Bosnia-Herzegovina, and every village seems to have at least one gifted storyteller. At any social gathering, such as a birthday party or wedding, the storyteller will entertain with tales about the family, the village, the great days of Yugoslavia under Marshal Tito, or some great victory in the recent years of war.

The lifestyle in Bosnia's cities is not markedly different from that in other parts of Europe. Casual clothes are seen more often than business attire. Women wear more conservative clothes than Americans, but slacks or jeans are common, as are polo shirts and T-shirts. City residents are much more aware of life in other parts of Europe, including the latest films and songs. ATMs are visible, and there are Internet kiosks in many cafés.

FAMILY TIME People spend a lot of time with their families, and many families take an evening stroll in their neighborhood or in the city center. Nightlife is also popular. Bosnians enjoy the dance clubs and jazz clubs, movies, concerts, and cafés, although going out to dinner is not nearly as common as in the United States.

Until the civil war there was considerable mixing among Bosniaks, Serbs, and Croats. Through people's jobs, friendships, or university study, members of the three groups intermingled freely. Intermarriage became quite common; residential areas and apartment buildings became increasingly multiethnic. The war changed that atmosphere. People are now more clannish, and they cross ethnic-religious boundaries with reluctance.

In addition, members of each group tend to follow the rules of their religion more closely than in the past. Still, many people, on their own or through small organizations, are trying to restore contacts and rebuild a sense of trust. Everyone agrees that years of effort will be required and that Bosnia-Herzegovina may never get back to what was normal in 1991.

Women wearing mini-skirts or headscarves can be seen in Bosnia's cities.

71

A young girl in a refugee camp. Thousands of children, especially Bosniaks, spent time in detention camps, then refugee camps.

CHILDHOOD

Although Bosnia has returned to peacetime life, for many children the nightmare of the war has not ended. UN officials estimate that more than half the country's children suffered severe trauma from the war and its aftermath. Girls as young as 9 were victims of beating and assault; many children were orphaned and many more had no homes to return to.

The UN Children's Fund (UNICEF) and other UN agencies have worked with private organizations such as Oxfam and the Save the Children (UK) fund to provide medical care and counseling. Every effort is made to locate missing family members and to arrange adoptions for orphans. Progress has been made, but authorities feel that healing will take many more years.

EDUCATION

Rebuilding Bosnia's schools has been a mammoth undertaking. Many schools were destroyed, especially in Muslim areas, where they were

favored targets of artillery and bombs. As the schools were being rebuilt, the UN Office of the High Representative for Bosnia-Herzegovina created a huge controversy by trying to rid schoolbooks of anything that could be considered "hatred speech" or "inflammatory content." While the motive was good, carrying out the policy created what amounted to dangerous censorship of art, literature, and music.

In Muslim-controlled regions, which are roughly 30 percent of the country, the committee struck down everything that seemed even remotely anti-Muslim. Reproductions of works of art with heroic war scenes were removed from textbooks and so was the Yugoslav national anthem. Critics of this policy argue that even Bosnian history is being rewritten to strike out events that might be troublesome to one group or another.

Once the controversy over textbooks started, leaders of ethnic/religious groups decided that their group would use separate textbooks. Thus, Bosniaks learn from "domestic" textbooks, which include Islamic symbols—even on the cover. Croat and Serb children read books that

School is compulsory and free for children aged 7 to 15. Many then go on to four years of secondary school.

make their ethnic group the heroes of Bosnian history. Many people feel that these trends will simply splinter the society further, and a number of efforts are under way to find a better approach.

One program, sponsored by several international agencies, is called Let Us Play. Soccer leagues and other after-school games are designed to encourage children from all three groups to participate in integrated sports. Another program—Education to Build Bosnia-Herzegovina— offers scholarships and other funds to improve educational opportunities. In spite of the many difficulties, there are signs of progress. Considering that in the past, Bosnian peasants were isolated from the world and had an antiquated lifestyle, the fact that roughly 90 percent of the people today are literate is encouraging.

INTERNATIONAL SUPPORT

Postwar Bosnia-Herzegovina has received an extraordinary amount support from a number of international institutions. The World Bank

Group met with Bosnian youth organizations in September 2004 to discuss the role of youth in the continuing reconstruction effort. Giacomo Filibeck, president of the European Youth Forum commented, "Investing in youth and in youth organizations is an obligation if we want to create a better society and a sustainable future."

The Center for Balkan Development (formerly Friends of Bosnia), a network of more than a thousand people in the United States, Canada, and Europe, continues its efforts to help all the former Yugoslav nations to rebuild. The focus of the organization is to educate Americans and Europeans about the plight of the Balkans and to work toward permanent solutions to the economic troubles of the region.

While the people of Bosnia are thankful for international assistance of all kinds, they understand that they must become self-sufficient in order to succeed. Foreign aid must be replaced with local and foreign private investments. Since the World Bank started operating in Bosnia-Herzegovina, the country has made great strides toward political and economic stability.

RELIGION

RELIGIOUS DIFFERENCES APPEAR to be at the heart of Bosnia's deep and bitter divisions. The civil war, which claimed an estimated 200,000 lives, certainly pitted Orthodox Serbs and Catholic Croats against the country's Muslims. The Muslims suffered the greatest loss of life and destruction of property.

There is more to the splintering of Bosnia-Herzegovina than religion, however. The rift has its roots in Communist rule, during which many of Bosnia's Islamic institutions were closed down, and many Serbs and Croats left the country because of the poor economy. People have not fought or argued over beliefs, claiming that one group's way of worship is superior. In fact, few people seemed to be deeply devout. Journalists and social scientists report that the religious differences are little more than labels for deeply felt nationalistic strivings.

Bosnian Serbs, for instance, want to restore the greatness of Yugoslavia, but as a Serbian state without Muslims or Croats. Since all three groups are basically the same in language and physical appearance, the one difference that stands out is the religious one.

As the conflict among the groups escalated, people began to see the other groups' religious practices as unpleasant at first, and eventually as hateful. Once the war started, people fought with great ferocity to destroy the symbols—as well as the people—associated with the hated religions, or to defend their own religious community from atrocities committed by the enemy.

Above: **An Orthodox priest conducts the funeral of a civil war casualty in Sarajevo.**

Opposite: **An Orthodox cathedral located In the center of Sarajevo.**

THE THREE RELIGIONS

Now that the war is over, many Bosnians are searching for ways to heal the deep divisions. But the death and destruction, the shattered lives and battered homes have left scars that will take many years to heal.

Christianity and Islam are two of the world's major religions, along with Hinduism, Judaism, and Buddhism. Christianity, in turn, is divided into three branches—Roman Catholic, Eastern Orthodox, and Protestant.

The three religions most practiced by Bosnians and Herzegovinians are Islam (40 percent), Eastern Orthodoxy (31 percent), and Roman Catholicism (15 percent).

EASTERN ORTHODOXY

In the fifth century A.D., as the Western Roman Empire fell to barbarian invasions the pope remained the head of the church in Rome, but the bishop, or patriarch, at Constantinople became the head of the Eastern Orthodox Church. The Eastern Empire, known as the Byzantine Empire, continued to exist for a thousand years after the fall of Rome, and during those centuries, the two Churches drifted farther apart. The split deepened over interpretation of the Holy Trinity.

While the patriarch has always been the head of the Eastern Orthodox Church, the churches in each country have been quite independent. In Bosnia-Herzegovina and Serbia, the institution is called the Serbian Orthodox Church. (Other branches are the Greek Orthodox and the Russian Orthodox.) In Bosnia-Herzegovina, there are bishops at Mostar, Banja Luka, and Tuzla.

As the Orthodox Church service has evolved, it has become very different from the Catholic service. Probably the most notable difference is that the Orthodox service is far more ornate, reaching all the senses through rich colors, elaborate ceremonies, Eastern music, and incense. The Orthodox Church also has many icons—formal paintings of Jesus, Mary, and many saints. Praying to an icon is considered the same as praying to the person pictured.

Left: **A Serbian woman prays in an empty Orthodox church in Sarajevo.**

Opposite: **This Serbian-Byzantine church in Gracanica is the only surviving building of the 14th-century Gracanica monastery. The rest of the monastery was destroyed by war.**

Above: **Muslim women and children pray at a refugee camp in Stobrec.**

Opposite: **A Janissary commander. Periodically, the Ottoman Turks selected a number of Christian boys between the ages of 10 and 20 and sent them to Istanbul for rigorous training in a palace school where they usually became loyal to the Ottoman regime and to Islam. Many of the best students became administrators in the Ottoman Empire. Others made up an elite guard called the Janissary Corps.**

ISLAM

Islam was founded by the Arab prophet Muhammad in the seventh century A.D. The holy book of Islam—the Koran—is regarded as "the Word of Allah (God)." Muslims share some beliefs with Jews and Christians, especially the belief in one God. They also accept Old Testament prophets, such as Abraham and Moses, and think of Jesus as another prophet, with Muhammad being the last and greatest of the prophets.

The Five Articles of Islamic Faith involve belief in one God; angels; the revealed books; the prophets; and the Day of Judgment. Believers are expected to practice the Five Pillars of Islam: to recite the profession of faith at least once; to observe the five daily calls to collective public prayer; to pay the *zakat* (purification) tax to support the poor; to fast daily from daybreak to sunset during the holy month of Ramadan; and to perform, if they are able to, the *hajj* (pilgrimage) to the holy city of Mecca in Saudi Arabia at least once in their life.

Muslims everywhere consider themselves members of a single worldwide community. In practice, however, there are differences from country to country, and there are differences between the two main branches of Islam—Sunni and Shiite.

When the Ottoman Turks conquered much of the Balkans in the late 15th century, they established a policy of tolerance toward other religions. Jews, however, were given special consideration and were often appointed to high administrative posts. Christians, while tolerated, soon learned that they could rise in the government or society only if they converted. There was also a good deal of discrimination. Christians, for instance, could not wear extravagant clothing or the color green. They were taxed more heavily than Muslims, and they could not build new churches without permission. There were also many petty forms of discrimination, such as having to dismount when a Muslim rode by. During the civil war many Serbs recalled these hated policies and used them to fuel the atrocities they inflicted upon Muslims.

ROMAN CATHOLICISM

Most Croats are Roman Catholic, as are the people of neighboring Croatia. Church missionaries began converting Slavic groups in the fifth century A.D. The Catholic Church is headed by the pope in Rome, assisted by bishops and archbishops around the world. The pope is regarded as the successor of Saint Peter, the leader of the Apostles, and is seen as the highest authority in the religion. The Bosnian archdiocese is in Sarajevo, and there are bishops in Mostar and Banja Luka.

Most Croats, and the few Catholic Serbs, attend Mass on Sunday, and a few go to daily Mass. They receive Holy Communion—the wafer and wine transformed during Mass into the body and blood of Jesus Christ. Other sacraments include baptism, confession, marriage, anointing of the sick, and last rites. Catholics believe in the Holy Trinity.

A Catholic woman confesses to a priest in the town of Medjugorje, where many believe the Virgin Mary has been appearing since 1981.

THE APPARITIONS AT MEDJUGORJE

At 6 P.M. on June 24, 1981, six Croat children were on a hill called Crnica, near the town of Medjugorje, when they were startled by a vision. What they saw was a beautiful young woman holding an infant. Frightened, the children ran away, but four of them returned the next day with two other children. The apparition returned, and this pattern was repeated for several days.

Word spread among the hill towns, and crowds began to follow the children. On the fifth day the lady spoke, telling the children that she was Mary, the mother of Jesus, and that she was bringing a message of love, urging people to work for peace and to pray to God for peace. An estimated 10,000 people were there that day, but apparently only the children could see or hear her. As the appearances continued, however, others have been able to see her and hear the message. The Catholic Church had the children examined, and they were found to be in good health—mentally and physically—but Church authorities remained reluctant to sanction the appearances as miracles.

Since 1981 the phenomenon at Medjugorje has continued to fascinate Catholics and non-Catholics from all over the world. The six visionaries, now in their 30s, still see the apparitions, and a few have traveled widely to tell of their experiences. A shrine has been built near the site *(above)*, and tour buses bring hundreds of pilgrims every day, even though travel was restricted between 1992 and 1995. Many believe that the Medjugorje region was saved from war damage by the presence of the Blessed Virgin.

THE BOGOMILS

Around the year A.D. 1180, a strong-willed ruler named Kulin took the title of *ban* (viceroy) and established a kingdom that covered much of Bosnia-Herzegovina. His political influence did not last long, but his religious ideas did. He declared himself a convert to Bogomilism—a Christian sect started by a Bulgarian monk named Bogomil. Bogomilism was one of several splinter sects that emerged during the Middle Ages, and it spread over many European and Asian provinces of the Byzantine Empire. Many Bosnians, including nobles, were attracted to it, and for a time it was known as the Bosnian Church.

The basic idea of Bogomilism was that the world was governed by the conflict between good and evil, and that evil ruled the affairs of humans. The Bogomils were ascetic, led simple lives, and kept away from indulgences such as marriage and drinking wine. They also held certain beliefs which were different from the traditional Catholic ones.

The Roman Catholic Church declared Bogomilism a heresy and sent Dominican friars to Bosnia to abolish the sect. Despite these efforts and the death of Kulin in 1204, Bogomilism continued through the 15th century before it finally died out.

GHOSTLY RELICS OF THE PAST

People traveling through Bosnia-Herzegovina are often fascinated—and puzzled—by monumental tombstones scattered throughout the countryside. There are about 60,000 of the gray stone markers, called *stecci*, dating back as far as the 12th century.

For a time, historians thought they were connected to the Bosnian Church, especially the strand called Bogomil. But historical evidence now suggests that the *stecci* were erected by followers of the Eastern Orthodox and Roman Catholic churches as well as the Bosnian.

About 10,000 of these ancient tombstones have decorations and a few have inscriptions. The designs include spirals, rosettes, vine leaves with grapes, and crescent moons, as well as some with figures. The most famous of the figures is of a man with his right hand raised *(above)*, as if in a gesture of loyalty. So far, no one has been able to interpret the markings, and the mystery of the *stecci* continues.

SARAJEVO'S MOST FAMOUS DOCUMENT

In 1492, as Christopher Columbus set out on his incredible voyage of discovery, the rulers of Spain—King Ferdinand and Queen Isabella—expelled all Jews from their kingdom. The Jews of Spain had lived under Muslim rule for several hundred years, so most of the refugees went to other parts of the Muslim world, including Bosnia, which was part of the Ottoman Empire.

The Jews who settled in Sarajevo brought with them a manuscript that is now the city's most famous cultural artifact. The manuscript is a 14th-century Haggadah—a book that describes the prayers and text to be used in celebrating Passover, the joyous holiday celebrating the Jews' escape from Egypt under the leadership of the patriarch Moses. The document is on display at the Zemaljski Muzej.

The oldest Jewish Sephardic Haggadah in the world is on public display in Sarajevo for the first time after a decade of repairs by international experts. The 109-page manuscript, rescued twice from war in recent decades, is regarded to be one of the most valuable Haggadahs in the world.

Sarajevo

**Dubrovnik
Split
Čapljina**

Sajam

LANGUAGE

THE PEOPLE OF BOSNIA-HERZEGOVINA have spoken basically the same language for more than a thousand years. The language—Serbo-Croatian—is also spoken in Croatia and in Serbia. The common language has not been a unifying force, however; instead, each group claims to have a separate language. The Bosniaks say they are speaking Bosnian; Croats call what is essentially the same language Croatian; and the Serbs refer to their language as Serbian. The three languages may have some differences with regard to pronunciation and vocabulary, but these are minor and speakers of the languages have little problem understanding each other. Serbo-Croatian has also been influenced by Islam and the Turkish occupation. Linguists estimate that more than 6,000 Serbo-Croatian words have Turkish origins.

Above: **A snack and news kiosk caters to passersby. The sign is written in the Latin alphabet, which is used in the Croatian and Bosnian languages. Serbian uses Cyrillic script.**

Opposite: **Road signs point the way in Mostar.**

The few thousand Roma still living in Bosnia usually speak Romany. This language traces its roots to northern India sometime before A.D. 1000. Over the centuries it has picked up loanwords from a dozen countries. Even though there is no history of Gypsy literature or writing, there is a rich oral tradition of songs and folktales. A number of writers in Bosnia and other Balkan countries have written tales and poems about Gypsies, using Serbo-Croatian or other Balkan languages.

Many people in Bosnia-Herzegovina also speak German, almost always as a second language. This practice developed during the 1970s and 1980s, when thousands of workers in economically troubled Yugoslavia were allowed to become temporary workers in the booming economy of West Germany. Many people today, especially young Bosnians, use English as a second language.

ONE LANGUAGE, TWO ALPHABETS

In A.D. 863, two brothers—Cyril and Methodius—were sent to the Czech lands by the patriarch of the Eastern Orthodox Church. The two monks were brilliant scholars and linguists, and their mission was to Christianize the southern Slavs. To acquaint the Slavic-speaking peoples with the Bible, they invented an alphabet, now called Cyrillic, based on the Greek alphabet. Since Slavic languages were rich in sounds, the brothers found they needed 43 letters, a number that has since been reduced.

The brothers were made saints in both the Eastern Orthodox and Roman Catholic branches of Christianity for Christianizing many Slavic peoples and for influencing the cultural development of those peoples. Together, Saint Cyril and Saint Methodius have the title of "the apostles of the Slavs."

A sign bears a Serbo-Croation message in Cyrillic with the English translation underneath.

CYRYLLIC LETTERS

The writing systems of Serbian are phonetic—that is, every letter is pronounced and the sound represented by that letter does not change from word to word. There is some variation in where the stress is placed in a word, but the one general rule is that the stress, or accent, is never on the last syllable, and in most words it is on the first vowel.

English letters	Cyrillic	Pronunciation	English letters	Cyrillic	Pronunciation
Aa	Аа	a in father	Ll	Лл	l in leg
Bb	Бб	b in bed	Mm	Мм	m in moon
Cc	Цц	ts in cats	Nn	Нн	n in night
Dd	Дд	d in door	Oo	Оо	o in open
Ee	Ее	e in bet	Pp	Пп	p in page
Ff	Фф	f in fire	Rr	Рр	r in room
Gg	Гг	g in goose	Ss	Сс	s in sun
Hh	Хх	h in human	Tt	Тт	t in time
Ii	Ии	ee in need	Uu	Уу	oo in spoon
Jj	Јј	y in yes	Vv	Вв	v in van
Kk	Кк	k in kid	Zz	Зз	z in zulu

A number of letters and pairs of letters have special sounds, especially when there is an accent mark. Here are some of the special pronunciations:

Latin script	Cyrillic	Pronunciation	Latin script	Cyrillic	Pronunciation
Čč	Чч	ch in cheese	Đđ	Ђђ	dg in badge
Dž dž	Џџ	j in jeep	Šš	Шш	sh in ship
Ćć	Ћћ	in ciao (as in Italian greeting)	Žž	Жж	s in vision
			Lj lj	Љљ	li in million
			Nj nj	Њњ	ny in canyon

The Cyrillic alphabet is still used in Russian, Ukrainian, and Bulgarian, as well as in the Serbian variant of Serbo-Croatian. Cyrillic remains the official alphabet of the Serbian Republic, and is also used in Macedonia. Croats and Bosniaks continue to use the Roman alphabet, the same alphabet that is used throughout Europe and the Americas. The box on this page shows the Cyrillic alphabet, with the 31 letters used in Macedonia and much of former Yugoslavia.

PRONUNCIATION

Both Serbo-Croatian, using the Roman alphabet, and Serbian, using the Cyrillic alphabet, are pronounced as they are written, and every letter is pronounced.

Although local dialects introduce variations in how words sound, there are a few general rules. The position of the stress in a word is never on the last syllable, and in most words the accent falls on the first vowel.

Some letters, especially those with accent marks and pairs of letters, have special sounds. The pronunciation of some of these special letters is given in the box below, along with some words and phrases.

SOME SPECIAL LETTERS

č	sounds like the ts in *cats*
c	like the ch in *cello*
ć	like the tch in *latch*
dz	like the j in *just*
j	like the y in *young*
s	like the sh in *mush*
z	like the s in *pleasure*

SOME WORDS

selo	village
pesma	song
reka	river
da	yes
ne	no
adravo	hello
dovidenja	goodbye

SOME PHRASES

Zovem se . . .	My name is . . .
Kako se zovete?	What's your name?
Gavorite li engleski?	Do you speak English?
Kada brod polazi?	What time does the boat leave?
Kada voz (or vlak in Croatian) dolazi?	What time does the train arrive?
Hvala.	Thank you.

REBUILDING THE NATIONAL LIBRARY

On August 25, 1992, an incendiary shell crashed into the National Library in Sarajevo *(right)*, engulfing it in flames. More shells followed over the next two days. Dr. Kemal Bakarsic, a librarian, described the result:

". . . All over the city, sheets of burned paper, fragile pages of gray ashes, floated down like a dirty black snow. Catching a page you could feel its heat, and for a moment read a fragment of text in a strange kind of black and gray negative, until, as the heat dissipated, the page melted to dust in your hand."

The destruction of the library was part of the Serb nationalists' plan to destroy all historical records of the country's Muslim past. The campaign of destruction began in the spring of 1992 and continued through summer. Even the date for the shelling of the National Library was planned—100 years after construction began.

The library, which included the University's documents, had been in a graceful Austro-Hungarian building on the edge of the Turkish Quarter (Bascarsija) overlooking the river. Bosnian authorities immediately decided to rebuild the structure as soon as the fighting stopped, and the government of Austria helped out by providing a new dome. By 2004 reconstruction was nearing completion, but much of the country's written history can never be restored. The National Library had held nearly 2 million volumes, including 155,000 rare books and manuscripts, as well as the nation's archive of newspapers and periodicals.

People in Sarajevo greet each other with a single kiss on each cheek.

NONVERBAL COMMUNICATION

Each of Bosnia's three ethnic/religious groups has certain ways of communicating without words that may be different from those of the other groups.

In the Serb Republic, for example, people greet one another with three kisses—first on the left cheek, then the right, and a third on the left. But in Sarajevo, and in other parts of the Bosniak-Croat Federation, the greeting is a single kiss on each cheek.

Customs also communicate. If you visit a Muslim's home, for instance, it would be insulting to keep your shoes on. Instead, the guest is expected to remove his or her shoes and wait for the host to provide a pair of slippers. Similarly, people leave their footwear outside before entering a mosque to maintain the mosque's cleanliness and sanctity.

ROMANY—LANGUAGE OF THE ROMA

The Roma lived in northern India until about A.D. 1000, and then began their worldwide wanderings. Their language, called Romany, is related to ancient Sanskrit, which was the language of northern India and is still in use among Hindu scholars. As the Roma moved through Europe, and eventually to every corner of the globe, they picked up bits of language from the countries in which they were living. A Balkan scholar named Franz von Miklosich has identified words from 13 European countries in modern Romany, including several hundred Serbo-Croatian words.

Over the past 1,000 years their language has been both a strength and a weakness for the Roma people (*below*). Since they have never had a homeland, they have been treated as outsiders wherever they live. This lack of legal status, combined with their distinctive physical appearance and fiercely independent lifestyle, has made them seem suspicious. Consequently, when local authorities heard them talking in a strange language, they often arrested them or considered them instruments of the devil. But the language was also a source of strength, since the Roma could communicate with one another, even in public, and what they said would be secret.

ARTS

LITERATURE, THE ARTS, and handicrafts all have a long and distinguished history in Bosnia-Herzegovina. As a nation at the crossroads between Europe and the Islamic world of the Middle East, several cultures have shaped and influenced that history. Music in Bosnia today, for example, ranges from ancient Turkish melodies to Balkan, or Slavic, folk songs to modern jazz and various kinds of rock music—and some kinds that mix several genres.

The country and its artists' minds are recognized far beyond the Balkan Peninsula. For instance, the Sarajevo Film Festival, held each August, draws filmmakers and actors from all over the world, and the city's Poetry Days has become one of the great international gatherings of poets. In addition, a number of Bosnian crafts, such as metalworking and weaving, are world renowned.

LITERATURE AND POETRY

In the 18th century Abbe Forte, the head of an Italian monastery, brought a long folktale in poetry form from Bosnia to Italy. This lament, or elegy, was to have a profound influence on literature and poetry throughout Europe. For instance, Germany's great author Johann Wolfgang von Goethe discovered it on a trip to Italy in the 1780s and not only translated it into German but also used it as a model for his own epic story of a love turned tragic by a failure in communication. English poet Lord Byron was also influenced by the folk poem titled *Hasanaganica* (*The Wife of Hasan Aga*)—in his poem of love gone awry, *Don Juan*.

Above: **French literary television program host Bernard Pivot visits the library in Sarajevo to witness efforts to rebuild it.**

Opposite: **A metal craft souvenir shop.**

95

HOMEGROWN WRITERS In the 19th century Bosnian writers played an important part in the growing movements for independence, using their literary powers to attack rule by outsiders—the Ottoman Turks. Another monk, Ivan Frano Jukic, started the country's first literary journal, *Bosanski Prijatelj* (*Bosnian Friend*), which spread the voice of protest throughout the Slavic countries.

The 20th century was a time of great literary creativity throughout the country. Bosniak, Serb, and Croat writers dealt with their own group's nationalistic aspirations and the need to drive out foreign influences—both Turkey and Austria-Hungary. Mesa Selimovic and Ivo Andriç were Bosnians, and both wrote novels describing the evils of repressive governments. And in spite of their Bosnian roots, both were associated with the drive to create a greater Yugoslavia that would be a blending of all three groups.

Ivo Andriç is widely regarded as the greatest Bosnian author and one of the towering novelists of the 20th century. As a nationalist who favored the creation of an independent Yugoslavia, he was jailed in 1918 on suspicion of involvement in the assassination of the Austrian archduke—the event that proved to be the match that ignited World War I. While in prison, Andriç began writing prose, gaining international fame for *Ex Ponto* (1918), a long, lyrical piece. Following his release from prison, he became a diplomat for the newly created Yugoslavia and published a short novel, *The Trip of Alija Djerzelez*, in 1920.

Andriç really hit his stride during World War II with two outstanding novels: *Travnicka hronika* (1945; published in English as *Bosnian Story*,

Ivo Andriç was born on the outskirts of Travnik on October 10, 1892. He studied philosophy in Austria, earned his doctorate, and gained a solid reputation as a poet.

1959); and *Na Drini cuprija* (1945; *The Bridge on the Drina*, 1959). Although his diplomatic work had taken him to Berlin, Rome, Bucharest, and other European capitals, his best writing drew on the rich variety of ethnic types in his native country. His novels, including the later *The Woman of Sarajevo*, explored Bosnia's history and the clash between East and West throughout that history. In 1961 he was awarded the Nobel Prize for Literature, the highest award an author can achieve. His work was praised by the Nobel Prize committee for its "epic force" and for the "great beauty and purity" of his language.

In spite of his great fame, Andrić has been severely criticized—mostly by Bosniaks, who felt his writing was anti-Muslim. Federation authorities have removed his novels from many libraries and schools. In 2002 the Travnik house where he lived, which had been turned into a museum devoted to his life story, was closed.

Bosnian novelist Ivo Andriç *(second from right)* **stands with four other Nobel Prize winners at the Stockholm Concert Hall, Sweden, in 1961. On his left is physicist Robert Hofstadter, while on his right** *(from right to left)* **are physician Georg von Bekesy, biochemist Melvin Calvin, and physicist Rudolf Mossbauer.**

20TH CENTURY VISUAL ARTS

At the end of the 19th century, with the arrival of Austro-Hungarian rule in Bosnia, the visual arts began to show influence of contemporary Europe. Young artists traveled throughout Europe, studying the styles of expressionism and impressionism. The 1950s brought to light a number of conceptual artists, including Braco Dimitrijevic. Cultural life in Bosnia's cities flourished through the 1960s and 1970s. Many institutions, including the Sarajevo Fine Arts Academy were established at this time.

During the siege of Sarajevo (1992–96) the artistic community made a concerted effort to continue working. It was possible to attend art exhibitions, as well as theatrical and musical events, throughout the war. In spite of Bosnia's wartime isolation from the international art scene, several art institutions were formed at this time, such as the Sarajevo Center for Contemporary Arts, a nonprofit organization that deals with the promotion and development of the country's contemporary visual arts.

Wartime destruction led to a lack of gallery space in Sarajevo. As a result, some artists use the city itself as their exhibition space. So-called public, site-specific art can be found throughout Sarajevo. These and other creative solutions will allow the arts to flourish in the 21st century.

FILM

One of Europe's great film directors, Bosnian Emir Kusturica, has had experiences similar to Andriç's. Kusturica, a Muslim, set his films in Sarajevo. He won the Golden Lion Award at the 1981 Venice Film festival for the film *Do You Remember Dolly Bell?* His reputation soared in 1984 when his film *When Father Was Away on Business* was nominated for an Academy Award as the year's best foreign film. But *The Underground*, considered his greatest film, was condemned in Sarajevo for being anti-Muslim. Angry and frustrated, Kusturica left the city and, as of 2003, has not returned.

Another outstanding filmmaker is Danis Tanovic. Born in Sarajevo, Tanovic made a striking film of the war, actually shooting the scenes in Slovenia and Italy because it was safer. The film, *No Man's Land*, is the story of two soldiers—a Serb and a Muslim—during the siege of Sarajevo. It won the Golden Palm Award in the 2001 Cannes Film Festival and an Academy Award as Best Foreign Film in 2002.

Above: **Film director Emir Kusturica** *(center)* **poses with cast members Natasa Solac** *(left)* **from Serbia and Montenegro and Slavko Stimac from Croatia during a press event for his film,** *Life is a Miracle,* **at the 57th Cannes Film Festival in 2004.**

Opposite: **A lioness walks amongst reproductions of famous paintings in an unconventional art exhibition by Bosnian artist Braco Dimitrijevic in Paris, France.**

MUSIC

Music in Bosnia-Herzegovina is such a delightful mixture of the old and the new, the West and the East, that it almost defies description. Country music, for example, has a variety of musical types that combine old-time folk songs with newer sounds. A traditional type of song, called *ravne pesme* (RAHV-nay PEE-es-mee), is very flat, almost tuneless; in its more modern guise, called *ganga* (GHAN-gah), it sounds to the uninitiated like someone shouting a rap song. Hearing more of either *ravne pesme* or *ganga* does not help a great deal, because the listener soon discovers that the same words are being sung to different tunes.

During the 45 years of Communist rule the government did not approve of Western music—that is, the music of western Europe and the United States. In fact, much of the time this "decadent" music was not allowed—on the radio or in live performances. The government did encourage folk music, and those traditional songs and melodies have been passed down from one generation to the other and remain very popular today.

MUSICAL INSTRUMENTS These also represent a mixture, primarily a blending of West and East. The traditional folk songs of rural villages are often played on unusual instruments, such as a Bosnian wooden flute or a bagpipe called a *diple* (deep-LAY).

Traditional urban music, like the rural folk songs, has an Oriental or Middle Eastern sound. These songs are sometimes difficult to perform because there can be more than one musical note for each syllable. This is called melismatic singing. But performers are able to work miracles with a remarkable one-string fiddle called a *gusla* (GOOS-lah). For centuries the gusla has been used to accompany a storyteller narrating and singing an epic poem. The most popular folk songs, both rural and urban, are called

Nine-year-old Bosnian Mario Miletic plays a violin in front of his class in a music school in a village near Medjugorje.

U2 lead singer Bono *(left)* holds a child on his lap and sits next to Italian opera tenor Luciano Pavarotti *(right)* as they watch youths perform in Mostar. Pavarotti and Bono were in Mostar for the opening of the Pavarotti Music Centre.

sevdalinka (SEV-DAHL-leen-kay). These are highly emotional love songs, usually telling of the great tragedy of a love lost or, occasionally, of finding one's great love.

Since 1990 the music of the West has become increasingly popular. Young people flock to discos and jazz clubs to dance or just to listen to the latest European and U.S. hits. In the 1980s a Bosnian rock group called Bijeto Dugme was hugely popular throughout the Balkans, but their success was cut short by the civil war.

Today, one of the most popular places in Bosnia is Mostar's Pavarotti Music Center. The music center was created in 1997 mostly through charitable contributions to provide a place for the children of Bosnia to learn about, perform, and enjoy music. It was conceived as a haven to escape the physical and emotional aftermath of war. The center's mission is to bring music to the people of Bosnia, "not because it is the complete answer, but because in some way it may fill that void left by war. Surely this is the nature of building peace."

DANCE

In communist Yugoslavia, traditional folk dancing was sponsored by the state and there were more then 300 amateur groups. Today, Bosnian traditions are perhaps the least known of all the regional folk dances of former Yugoslavia.

A popular folk dance called *nijemo kolo* (NEE-YAY-moh KOH-loh) is performed without music. Instead, the rhythmic stamping of feet and the jingling of coins sewn into women's aprons or skirts accompany this dance, which is performed with great speed and dexterity. In many folk dances men and women form separate lines, similar to square dancing or line dancing.

As with music, interest in these traditional dance forms is diminishing due to the influence of the modern era and Western popular culture.

A Bosnian troupe performs a folk dance at a function.

103

CRAFTS

Bosnia-Herzegovina has a long, proud handicraft tradition, particularly in textiles, metalworking, and woodworking, all dating back to the rule of the Ottoman Turks in the 15th and 16th centuries. In textiles, some craftspeople worked in their cottages, while others had separate stalls or shops in a domed building called a *bezistan* (BEZZ-ih-stahn).

WEAVING Bosnian weavers employed techniques and designs from Persia (modern Iran) to create exquisite rugs and wall hangings. Using a design drawn on paper called a cartoon, the workers used painsta-

Bags, prayer mats, and rugs showcase the talent of Bosnian weavers.

king care to weave the complex design into wool cloth. Until the late 1800s only natural dyes were used—from plants, such as indigo, from minerals, such as ocher, and from animal life, including certain insects. These natural dyes produced many subtle shadings that artificial dyes could not duplicate, and the resulting colors were rich and long-lasting.

Another unique feature of the weaving is the hand knotting of the yarn around the warp yarns. Creating the luxurious pile of a true Persian, or Oriental, rug could require more than 2,000 knots per square inch! On rare occasions Bosnian weavers worked with exotic fabrics such as velvet or silk, often with threads of silver and gold.

A Bosnian woman designs a carpet in a textile mill.

Above: **Copperwork has flourished in Bosnia-Herzegovina since Ottoman rule. Sarajevo and Banja Luka were known as artisan centers during the Ottoman period.**

Opposite: **Although Islam discourages the representation of living things in art, contemporary artists in Bosnia are exploring new limits, as these wooden sculptures testify.**

Page 108: **The ceiling and walls of the Koski Mehmed Pasha Mosque are painted with intricate patterns.**

EMBROIDERY Bosnian craftspeople were also famous for their embroidery, stitching colorful designs on women's blouses and aprons, men's traditional clothes, scarves and shawls, pillowcases, and other items.

The most common designs were geometric patterns, sometimes incorporating plant life, such as blossoms, leaves, and stems. Bosnian women learn to embroider at a very young age, and the needlework is very much part of the culture.

METALWORKING In Oriental-style bazaars in Mostar, Sarajevo, and other cities, skilled metalworkers sit in their small, cluttered shops hammering elaborate designs in brass or copper to be used for household items, such as coffeepots, trays, bowls, and jewelry. Some towns are known for the specialization of their metalworkers. They sometimes work on larger metal items, such as doors and gates. Some metalworkers specialize in filigree—using thin, twisted wires of copper, silver, or gold. Others focus on techniques such as embossing—creating a raised design.

WOODWORKING This is another highly refined craft. Ornate carvings are used in the interior of houses, including moldings, doors, furniture, and paneling. Mosques and minarets also have elaborate wood carving. As in other forms of Islamic art, there are no representations of humans, but floral and animal shapes are common, as are designs based on calligraphy.

POTTERY In the Bosnian countryside traditional potters produce pieces using an ancient method that is extinct elsewhere. The mineral calcite is added to the clay, which is formed into pots on a hand-operated wheel. The pots are often fired on a bonfire. This technique died out throughout the rest of Europe several centuries ago. The pots are in great demand for use in traditional Bosnian cooking. Potters using this method can still be found working in several towns in Bosnia-Herzegovina. In Ljesevo, near Sarajevo, a different style is represented where fancier pots are kiln-fired and decorated.

THE INFLUENCE OF ISLAM

Ever since Islam arrived in the country in the 16th century via Ottoman rule, the religion has had a strong influence on arts and crafts, although less so in Bosnia-Herzegovina than in other parts of the Muslim world. In Bosnia, that influence is most noticeable in the visual arts and several crafts. In painting, for example, humans and animals are not to be represented, and this ban extends to crafts, such as weaving and embroidery.

Many craftspeople work with a design called arabesque, in which one leaf or blossom and vine grows out of another and then another with no apparent beginning or end. Artists and crafts workers have an aversion to open spaces, so the arabesque offers a natural solution to this.

Islam provides artistic minds with rich opportunities in the decorating of mosques, minarets, and other Muslim structures. A mosque is likely to have beautifully carved wood for the niche (mihrab) pointing to Mecca, and also for staircases, balustrades, and the stand for the Koran. Other artistic opportunities include bronze candlesticks with inlaid ornamentation and also design and color variations in woven prayer mats.

LOST TREASURES

The Islamic arts of Bosnia-Herzegovina were among the casualties of the civil war, 1992–95. In Sarajevo, for example, the Oriental Institute housed one of the most important collections of Islamic manuscripts in the world. In May 1992 Bosnian Serbs, determined to get rid of all evidence of Muslim culture, destroyed the institute and its collections. Thousands of documents from the days of Ottoman rule were burned, along with about 5,000 handwritten manuscripts in several different languages—Turkish, Arabic, Hebrew, Greek, and Persian.

The original documents are beyond recovery, but for about 40 years prior to the war, the institute encouraged other organizations to borrow copies on long-term loan and to reproduce them. Staff members are now contacting the borrowing institutions and have already replaced several hundred items.

Similar losses were sustained by the Museum of Herzegovina *(above)* and the Archives of Herzegovina. In these cases, however, the art and documents cannot be replaced, since there were no copies.

LEISURE

IN THE EARLY 21ST CENTURY Bosnians are again enjoying leisure activities that had been impossible through most of the 1990s. They avidly pursue traditional pastimes, ranging from vigorous activities, such as hunting and skiing, to more sedentary enjoyments, such as chess and card games. Many have also become enthusiastic about the leisure pursuits of the West, such as basketball, surfing the Internet, and in-line skating.

Bosnians spend a lot of time with their families, enjoying large meals on Sundays and holidays, usually followed by a walk through the downtown of their small cities. (Even Sarajevo, by far the largest city, has fewer than 500,000 people.)

People enjoy shopping, and even buying food seems more of a leisure activity than the typical American minivan excursion to a supermarket. In fact, supermarkets are rare because Bosnians prefer to stroll through open-air markets every day or two, buying only what they can carry home walking or riding the tram.

Shopping malls are a recent addition, especially in the rebuilt cities and suburbs. As in the United States and western Europe, young people like to hang out, but anything that looks like loitering is not approved of. Bands and theatrical groups often provide entertainment.

Bosnia's many forests, streams, and mountains provide ample opportunity for hunting, hiking, rafting, and skiing, among other activities.

Above: **A woman buys fruit from a stall at an open-air market in Bosnia. Bosnians visit such markets frequently to buy food.**

Opposite: **People bargain with traders over the prices of their goods at a street market in Sarajevo.**

HUNTING

Bosnia, like other mountainous regions of southeastern Europe, has been considered a sportsman's paradise for some 300 years. Wealthy Europeans and members of the nobility have come to this part of the Balkans to hunt several prized trophies, such as the ever-dangerous wild boar, European bison, and the Carpathian red deer, a large deer known for its huge antlers.

The popularity of hunting in these primitive-looking forests has contributed to the disappearance, or near disappearance, of some species. For instance, the aurochs, a large wild ox, is extinct, and the European bison, slightly larger than the North American species, was reduced to fewer than a dozen animals in private collections by the 1930s. These few have been used to start a new breeding herd, with some interbreeding with North American bison, but none have been reintroduced into the wild.

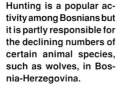

Hunting is a popular activity among Bosnians but it is partly responsible for the declining numbers of certain animal species, such as wolves, in Bosnia-Herzegovina.

In a strange way, the popularity of some game animals may contribute to their survival. The Herzegovinian brown bear, for example, is a big, lumbering creature that has retreated deep into the Dinaric Mountains. Income from hunting permits provides revenue that is helping to establish reserves to protect the remaining bears. In addition, conservation efforts have helped some hunted species make a comeback, including the lynx.

The hunting of game birds has also led to the decline of several species. The black grouse, for example, was hunted almost to extinction before conservation programs began to reverse the trend in the 1970s.

FISHING AND WATER SPORTS

The spectacular Bosnian scenery, with its challenging mountains and sparkling rivers, also draws people for fishing. Some remote fishing lodges have pampered guests for 100 years or more. In addition to rushing trout streams, Bosnia's two large lakes, Jablanicko Jezero and Busko Jezero, are considered outstanding for bass and other game fish.

The Una River attracts both fishing enthusiasts and white-water rafters.

UNUSUAL GAME FISH Bosnia also has some unusual fish that lure sports fishers who want to try something new. The huchen, for example, is a large troutlike fish that reaches lengths of 5 feet (1.5 m) and a weight of 110 pounds (50 kg). Other unusual game fish are the gudgeon and the catfishlike loach.

The rushing streams also draw white-water rafters from many countries. The Una River near Biha is famous for its long stretches of rapids. There was heavy fighting in and around Biha during the civil war, but nearly all the damage has been repaired and the area seems to be clear of landmines. The rafting season runs from May through October, and the Una Regatta is held for two weeks in July.

A group of boys enjoys playing ice hockey on a frozen stream in Bosnia-Herzegovina.

Soccer is a favorite sport in Bosnia-Herzegovina.

SPORTS

Bosnians enjoy a variety of individual and team sports. The selection of Sarajevo as the site for the 1984 Winter Olympics was recognition of the sports-mindedness of the people and the availability of natural sites for events like downhill and cross-country skiing. Only about 20 of the world's cities have been chosen for the Winter Games.

Skiing has long been popular in the region, and people can still enjoy the downhill slopes groomed for the Olympics. Sledding and ice-skating are also popular, and hockey is gaining a larger following every year.

The two great team sports are soccer and basketball. Soccer has been growing rapidly since the 1950s, and there are now three professional leagues—two from the Federation and one from the Serbian Republic. The Bosnian national team participates in the World Cup every four years, the world's most popular sports event. In the 2000 Euro Games the team finished a satisfactory fourth in its grouping of seven teams, and then began preparing for the 2002 World Cup.

TAKING GAMES TO THE STREETS Kids throughout the country play pickup games in parks, parking lots, fields, and in the streets. Many schools and clubs have teams. The televising of professional games and World Cup matches has contributed to the growing popularity of the sport.

Basketball is a late arrival in Bosnia-Herzegovina, and it is growing with remarkable speed. Backboards and rims (with or without nets) are appearing with increasing frequency in parks and on neighborhood utility poles. There are both professional and amateur teams, and people closely follow the careers of players who have made it to the U.S. National Basketball Association (NBA).

Other outdoor sports include skateboarding and in-line skates. Cycling is also popular, including road races similar to the Tour de France, which is an annual world cycling race.

Wealthy families enjoy horseback riding, and several communities in the north are known for both breeding and training horses. The famous Lipizzaner horses, introduced from Austria in the mid-1800s, are favorites both for pleasure riding and also for formal competitions in dressage—the highly skilled maneuvering of a horse in what has been called an equestrian ballet.

ENTERTAINMENT

The people of Bosnia-Herzegovina have been fond of American music for several generations. Even during the austere days of Communist rule, goodwill tours by Louis Armstrong and other great jazz figures were well received. By the 1980s all forms of American music were played in discos and jazz clubs. Young people flock to these places, usually for live music, although deejays are becoming more common.

While most Bosnians enjoy an evening out for music or espresso, eating out is not very popular. Restaurants in all price ranges are numerous, but these seem to be frequented more by tourists and diplomats than by locals, although exceptions are made to celebrate a special event. As in other countries, movies and television constitute the evening's entertainment for many Bosnians.

Above: **Bosnians chat with friends in a bar in Sarajevo.**

Opposite: **Basketball is a popular sport and is overseen by the Bosnia-Herzegovina Basketball Federation.**

FESTIVALS

THE PRESENCE OF THREE RELIGIONS in the country gives Bosnia a colorful array of festivals, holidays, and holy days. There are also several holidays that have been imported in recent years through travel or even Internet contact. Earth Day, with posters and picnics promoting environmental protection, is celebrated in several towns in early April, with e-mail linkages providing some publicity. Halloween is another recent import, with many kids copying costume ideas they see on television. The Roman Catholic Church has not objected but insists the day be called All Saints' Day.

Two religions will sometimes honor the same holiday, but in quite different ways. Both the Roman Catholic Church and the Eastern Orthodox Church celebrate Christmas and Easter, but their observances are quite different. Both also honor Saints Cyril and Methodius, but the Catholics honor them in April, the Eastern Orthodox in May.

Secular festivals are also varied. National Day for Bosnia-Herzegovina is March 1, for example, the date Bosnia separated from Yugoslavia. Bosnian Serbs do not honor this date, preferring their own holiday of November 25— the Day of the Republic.

In every religion, spring is a time to celebrate the renewal of life and the anticipation of a new crop year. For Serbs and Croats the celebration is Djurdjevdan, a time to celebrate the fertility and renewal of the land. The festival—complete with food, music, and dances—is most important in farming villages.

Above: **Calendars with pictures of political figures are pinned up for sale at a Banja Luka square during New Year celebrations.**

Opposite: **Bosnian men and women dance in traditional costumes.**

119

Muslim men stand in congregational prayer in Sarajevo at the end of Ramadan, the fasting month.

RELIGIOUS HOLIDAYS: ISLAM

Bosnia's Muslims—Bosniaks—have a number of Islamic holy days and other religious occasions that are not observed by Christians or Jews. For instance, five times each day Muslims hear the muezzin call them to worship, usually from a minaret (a tower normally attached to a mosque). On hearing the call, observant Muslims face in the direction of Mecca and recite their daily prayers.

The most important event in Islam is the month-long Fast of Ramadan —observed during the ninth month of the lunar calendar. It is the month when the Prophet Muhammad received the words of the Koran. Every day of the month is a time of prayer and reflection, and Muslims are expected to fast during daylight hours.

Ramadan is also a time to celebrate with family and friends. As soon as the sun goes down, Bosniaks break the fast with a prayer and a meal —the *iftar* (EEF-tar). The streets are filled with people visiting family and friends or enjoying Turkish coffee and baklava at an outdoor café.

When the month of fasting ends, on the first day of the month of Shawwal, there is a three-day holiday and celebration called Id-al-Fitr, the Feast of the Fast Breaking. This three-day celebration is also known as Baj'ram. People gather with family and close friends for three days of extended meals. Many Bosniaks exchange gifts, and a number of towns have street fairs, with food stalls and live music. The minarets are decorated with strings of electric lights.

A man offers sheep for sale as Bosnians prepare for Baj'ram.

SECULAR FESTIVALS

January 1 and 2	New Year's
January 9	Republika Srpska (Serb Republic)
February and March	Winter Festival
March 1	Independence Day
May 1	International Labor Day
November 25	National Day

Bosnian children wear party hats to celebrate Christmas. Members of the Eastern Orthodox church celebrate Christmas in early January instead of in December, like the Roman Catholics do.

RELIGIOUS HOLIDAYS: CHRISTIAN

Christmas and Easter are the principal religious holidays for all three branches of Christianity, although the forms of celebration differ. Bosnia's Roman Catholics, mostly Croats, celebrate Christmas much as Americans do, although with a good deal less commercialism. While families may have a Christmas tree, for example, decorations and gifts are more modest.

The Eastern Orthodox Christmas is slightly different, including the date, which is in early January rather than on December 25. There are also regional variations in the celebration. For instance, while many families cut a traditional pine or spruce for their Christmas tree, families in some regions choose a young oak for a Yule tree, or *badnjak* (BAHD-nyak). The oak symbolizes both the Cross on which Jesus was crucified and also the new life that will come in the spring. (The oak holds its leaves far longer than other trees, often until late in the winter.) The lower part of the trunk is cut and burned as a Yule log, while the branches are decorated with ribbons, fruit, and candy. Straw is spread around the base of the tree for the manger in which the baby Jesus was born, and more straw is spread around the festive table.

The Eastern Orthodox Easter is held from one to five weeks after the Catholic and Protestant Easter. The standard Easter greeting is "Christ is Risen." Orthodox families place an Easter cake in a basket, with painted eggs, butter, and cheese, and take it to the church for the priest's blessing

Bosnian Serbs also celebrate Krsna Slava—a sort of collective birthday, also called Saint George's Day in some parts of the country. Every family has a patron saint, usually a figure from far back in history. For more than half the families, Saint George is the family patron, and the saint's day is to commemorate the time when the family, or its tribal group, was baptized into the Orthodox faith. Bosnian Serbs celebrate the day with street fairs and music, as well as again taking holiday cakes to the local church for a priestly blessing.

An Orthodox priest gives sacraments during Easter services in a church in Sarajevo, the capital of Bosnia-Herzegovina.

FOOD

BOSNIAN FOODS TEND TO BE heavy and rich. As in other Balkan countries, the emphasis is on meat and potatoes or bread.

People usually shop every day or two. The open-air markets present a tempting array of aromas and colors. Shoppers select from open trays and crates of fruits, such as regionally grown apples, melons, plums, pears, and grapes as well as imported items such as bananas, oranges, and pomegranates. Similarly, vegetables are not prepackaged and people fill their shopping bags from sacks and boxes of cabbages, potatoes, salad produce, and various kinds of wild mushrooms. Meats, with lamb being the most popular, are purchased from a butcher's stall or shop.

Above: **Kosovo-Albanian refugee children rest after receiving food aid in the Rakovic refugee centre, near Sarajevo.**

Opposite: **People buy fruit and vegetables at a market in Sarajevo.**

The Bosnian version of fast food is *cevapcici* (CHAY-VAHP-chee-chee), which has been popular for nearly 500 years. *Cevapi* (che-VA-pee), for short, is a sausage made of ground lamb, or sometimes beef or pork, lots of spices, and grilled with onions. It is often grilled outdoors and served warm on *somun* (SO-moon), a thick pita bread.

If *cevapcici* is the Bosnian version of a hot dog, *pljeskavica* (PLYES-kah-veet-tzah) is something like a Balkan hamburger. Prepared much like *cevapi*, it is formed into patties, much like an American burger.

Breakfast (*dorucak,* DOE-ru-chak) is a hearty beginning to the day, and it is served early, with coffee, tea, or warm milk as an introduction. The typical breakfast would then consist of scrambled eggs, a soft white cheese, and bread with butter and jam or honey.

Lunch is the most substantial meal of the day. Most people eat with their family late in the afternoon, usually around two o'clock. Supper is normally a light meal, served around 8 P.M.

LUNCH The afternoon meal is likely to begin with a hearty homemade soup. This is followed by fish or meat, served with vegetables and salad, and then dessert. Probably the favorite main dish is *bosanski lonac* (BOSS-ahn-skee LON-atz)—layers of lamb, or beef, and vegetables, slow-roasted and served in a ceramic pot with a long, wide neck, something like a large flower vase. Other popular dishes include *burek* (BU-rek), a meat pie; *japrak* (YA-prak*)*, tasty cabbage rolls stuffed with ground lamb and rice; *sirnica* (SEER-nee-tsa), a flaky pastry filled with soft cheese; and *zeljanica* (zel-YA-nee-tsa), a spinach pie. These stuffed pastries and shish kebab, another favorite, represent the influence of Turkish cuisine.

Desserts are usually light, consisting of plain cake or pudding and fresh fruit. Plums are close to being the national fruit and are also used to make *rakija* (RA-kee-ya), a sweet brandy that can also be made with grapes. The former Yugoslavia was one of the world's largest producers of plums.

Baklava, a Turkish dessert, is well-liked in Bosnia-Herzegovina. It is made of layers of light, flaky pastry, filled with honey and chopped nuts.

A Bosnian woman serves desserts to her guest.

The most famous dessert in Bosnia-Herzegovina is baklava, which Bosnians eat only on special occasions. If you have eaten real baklava, you know why it is a special treat—because it is extra sweet and rich.

Tufahijia (tul-FA-hee-ya) is another very sweet dessert made from apples stuffed with chopped walnuts and topped with whipped cream. And a confection called Turkish Delight is as sticky as it is sweet.

For beverages, kids and young children drink milk or *kefir* (KE-feer), a thin yogurt drink, and occasionally soft drinks. All beverages are consumed after the main course. Adults have beer or wine, with many local varieties to choose from. Normally, Muslims do not drink alcoholic beverages, although this ban was not strictly observed in Bosnia before the civil war. After-meal drinks can be brandy, coffee, Turkish coffee, espresso, or a Bosnian tea called *salep* (SA-lep). Since the war, however, many Bosniaks have become more strict in their observance of Islamic laws, and some towns have passed laws against serving alcoholic drinks in restaurants and cafés.

PITA AND NATIONAL PRIDE

Although the spirit of nationalism has often divided the people of Bosnia, there are times that a patriotic spirit can pull all three ethnic-religious groups together. Their feelings about national foods provide one example: Bosnians are convinced that only their cooks know how to prepare pita *(below)*—the thin bread that is popular throughout the Mediterranean world. Bosnian journalist Nicholas S. Balamaci writes, "Everyone in America thinks pita is quintessentially Greek. And yet . . . according to the foremost authorities, pita is a [Bosnian] specialty that Greeks have only attempted to copy in the last century."

Not only is the bread original to Bosnians, at least on the Balkan Peninsula, but also its quality is superior to that of pita made in any other country. As Balamaci writes, " . . . our devotion to it is almost religious. And why not? It takes a good morning's work to roll out the pieces of dough, one by one, to make a good pita." People in other countries, Bosnians insist, tend to use ready-made dough, which is considered bad form and likely to be tasteless.

Is the Bosnian pride valid? Try the recipe for *zeljanica* (spinach pita) and see what you think.

BOSANSKI LONAC (BOSNIAN POT)

Many Bosnians think of Bosnian Pot as their national dish. It has the ingredients they love—lots of meat and potatoes, plus onion and garlic. This recipe will serve six to eight people.

1 small cabbage
3 carrots
3–4 large tomatoes
3–4 large potatoes
2 onions
2 or more cloves garlic, peeled and sliced

2 green bell peppers
2 pounds lamb (or beef), diced
½ tablespoon cooking oil
½ tablespoon vinegar
salt and pepper to taste

Dice all the vegetables. Combine everything (except the oil and vinegar) with the meat and seasonings in a large pot. (This is a great recipe for a Crock-Pot.) Add enough water to completely cover the mixture, then add the oil and vinegar. Cover and cook over low heat for two or three hours, until everything is well-done. Serve with pita bread.

ZELJANICA (SPINACH PITA)

This recipe is of Vlach origin. The Vlachs are a small ethnic group in Bosnia-Herzegovina and Albania. This recipe yields about 18 pieces.

2 10-ounce packages frozen spinach
1 pound (0.5 kg) cottage cheese (farmer cheese or Greek feta cheese can also be used), crumbled
4 eggs
1 cup butter, melted
dash of salt
4$\frac{1}{2}$–5 cups unbleached flour
2 teaspoons salt
2–2$\frac{1}{2}$ cups water

To make the filling

1. Prepare spinach according to package. Strain and let cool.
2. In a large bowl, combine prepared spinach, cheese, eggs, one tablespoon of the melted butter, and dash of salt. Set aside.

To make the crust

1. In a large bowl, sift $4^1/_2$ cups of flour.
2. Add two teaspoons salt, and mix with a fork.
3. Slowly add the water, and work dough with fingertips until it is smooth and elastic.
4. Knead for about 10 minutes, adding more sifted flour or more water, if needed. Try to keep the dough light and fluffy; if you knead too much, it will become tough.
5. Cover with a towel and let stand for 15 minutes.
6. Split the dough in half to form two pieces.
7. Sprinkle some flour on one piece of the dough, and roll it out until thin and about the size of a jelly roll pan (1inch by 14 inches by 12 inches or 2.5 cm by 36 cm by 31 cm).
8. Spread some of the melted butter on the dough, then refrigerate for about 15 minutes.
9. Repeat the same procedure with the second piece of dough.
10. When the dough is chilled, remove the first piece from the refrigerator.

To assemble

1. Sprinkle a little flour on the dough and roll it out more, so that it's about 1 inch (2.5 cm) bigger than the pan on all sides.
2. Butter the pan, and place the rolled-out dough in the pan.
3. Add the spinach filling, and spread it evenly.
4. Roll out the second piece of chilled dough so that it overlaps at least 1 inch (2.5 cm) on all sides of the pan. Place over the spinach filling, and tuck edges neatly into the side of the pan to form a thick crust.
5. Brush the remaining melted butter on the top.
6. Bake at 450°Fahrenheit (232°C) for 15 minutes, then lower the heat to 400°F (204°C) and bake for 15 minutes longer, or until golden brown and crispy.
7. Remove from oven and cut into squares.

CROATIA

A   B   C   D

1

●Bihac

REPUBLIKA

SRPSKA

●Banja Luka

●Tuzla

2

Vrbas

Zvornik●

●Travnik

●Kakanj

REPUBLIKA

Bosna

SRPSKA

BOSNIAC-CROAT

SARAJEVO

3

▲
Mt. Trebevic
(5,338 ft / 1,627 m)

FEDERATION

Buóko
Jezero

Mostar ●

▲ Zelena Gora
(6,900 ft / 2,103 m)

Drina

● Medjugorje

Neretva

▲
Lelija
(6,667 ft / 2,032 m)

ADRIATIC

DALMATIAN COAST

▲ Mt. Maglic
(7,881 ft / 2,387 m)

SEA

DINARIC
ALPS

SERBIA &

MONTENEGRO

4

N

International boundary
Inter-entity boundary
● Capital city

Feet   Meters
9,900   3,000
6,600   2,000
3,300   1,000
1,650   500
660   200
0   0

5

MAP OF BOSNIA

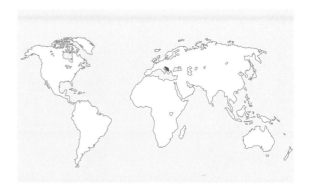

ECONOMIC BOSNIA

Natural Resources

- Bauxite
- Coal
- Hydroelectricity
- Lead
- Manganese
- Zinc

Services

- Airport
- Tourism

Manufacturing

- Chemicals
- Construction
- Food Processing
- Leather
- Textiles
- Wood Processing

Agriculture

- Grapes
- Livestock
- Maize
- Potatoes
- Rice
- Tobacco
- Wheat

ABOUT THE ECONOMY

ECONOMIC OVERVIEW

Bosnia and Herzegovina ranked next to The Former Yugoslav Republic of Macedonia as the poorest republic in the old Yugoslav federation. Warfare in Bosnia caused production to plummet from 1992 to 1995 and unemployment to soar. Implementation of privatization has been slow. In addition, postwar reconstruction assistance and humanitarian aid from the international community is declining.

GDP

US$6.2 billion (2002 estimate)

PER CAPITA INCOME

US$1,900 (2002 estimate)

GDP SECTORS

Agriculture 13 percent
Industry 40.9 percent
Services 46.1 percent

LAND AREA

19,735 square miles (51,129 square km)

LAND USE

Arable land 9.8 percent, forested land 36 percent

CURRENCY

Convertible mark, or marka, (BAM) launched in 1998
USD 1 = BAM 1.57

WORKFORCE

1.026 million

UNEMPLOYMENT RATE

About 40 percent (2002 estimate)

INFLATION RATE

3.5 percent (2002)

AGRICULTURAL PRODUCTS

Corn, wheat, vegetables, fruit, wine, beer, poultry, lamb, veal, beef, pork

MINERALS

Bauxite (aluminum), iron, coal

INDUSTRIES

Steel, mining, textiles, timber, oil refining

MAJOR EXPORTS

Oriental rugs, oil, timber

MAJOR IMPORTS

Food, electronic equipment, motor vehicles

MAIN TRADING PARTNERS

European Union, Yugoslavia, United States

PORTS AND HARBORS

Bosanski Brod

LEADING FOREIGN INVESTORS

United States, Italy, Germany, Hungary, Austria, Greece, Croatia, Slovenia

CULTURAL BOSNIA

Fehija Mosque
The Fehija Mosque in Bihac is an interesting combination of architectural styles in a mosque that was built out of an old Gothic church and retained the idea of tall stained-glass windows.

World War II Memorial
The huge white stone of this memorial in Banja Luka has a solemn dignity. The hill also offers a grand view of the city.

16th-century castle
This castle on the banks of the Vrbas River in Banja Luka hosts a music and drama festival every July.

Dobrinja
This modern suburb was built as the Athletes' Village for the 1984 Winter Olympics.

Gazi Husref-Bey Mosque
This classic, domed mosque in Sarajevo was built in 1531. The tall minaret has been rebuilt due to war damage.

Mount Bjelasnica
The mountain overlooking Sarajevo still has the ski slopes designed for the 1984 Winter Games.

Turkish Quarter
The Bascarsija, or old Turkish Quarter, in Sarajevo has narrow cobblestone streets and is famous for the shops of metalworkers.

Jajce
A brooding medieval fortress looms over the fertile Vrbas River valley. During World War II this was the headquarters for Tito's Partisan fighters battling the Germans.

Travnik
A medieval fort is the outstanding feature of this small city that was headquarters for Turkish governors for more than 400 years. This was also the birthplace of Ivo Andris, the great Bosnian novelist.

Apparition Hill
Southwest of Medjugorje, near Podbro village, a blue cross marks the spot where six children first saw the Virgin.

Stari Most
This bridge in Mostar was built by the Ottoman Turks in 1566, destroyed by Croat artillery in 1993, and rebuilt with international help in 2003.

Turkish House
Still standing after earthquakes and war, this house in Mostar is now nearly 400 years old. It contains Turkish-style rugs and finely carved wooden furnishings.

Karst terrain
In the southern and southwestern parts of Bosnia-Herzegovina are deep limestone depressions and caves that became known as a karst landscape. The name has since been applied to similar landscapes in other parts of the world.

St. James Church
Next to this church in Medjugorje is an information booth that has daily schedules and also printouts, in several languages, of the new message the Holy Mother gives to one of the visionaries on the 25th of each month.

ABOUT THE CULTURE

OFFICIAL NAME
Republic of Bosnia and Herzegovina

CAPITAL
Sarajevo

OTHER MAJOR CITIES
Mostar, Banja Luka, Bihac, Gacko, Medjugorge, Travnik

FLAG
Adopted in 1998. A yellow triangle on a blue field. The three sides (or points) of the triangle represent the three main ethnic groups—Bosnian Muslims (Bosniaks), Serbs, and Croats. The blue background represents Europe and the stars stand for the Council of Europe. The two half-stars represent the division of the country into the Federation of Bosnia-Herzegovina and the Serb Republic; these half-stars also represent the hope that the two entities can be united.

POPULATION
3,989,018 (July 2003 estimate)

POPULATION DENSITY
199 per square mile; 43 percent urban

POPULATION GROWTH RATE
0.5 percent (2004 estimate)

ETHNIC GROUPS
Bosniak 48 percent, Serb 37.1 percent, Croat 14.3 percent, other 0.6 percent

LIFE EXPECTANCY
70 years (male), 75 years (female)

TIME
Central European Time: Greenwich Mean Time plus one hour (GMT/UTC +0100)

RELIGIONS
Muslim 40 percent, Eastern Orthodox 31 percent, Roman Catholic 15 percent, Protestant 4 percent, other 10 percent.

LITERACY RATE
94 percent

OFFICIAL LANGUAGES
Croatian, Serbian, and Bosnian

EDUCATION
Free and compulsory, ages 7 to 15

NATIONAL HOLIDAY
Day of the Republic, November 25

LEADERS IN THE ARTS
Mesa Selimovic (writer), Ivo Andriç (writer), Emir Kusturica (film director)

TIME LINE

IN BOSNIA-HERZEGOVINA	IN THE WORLD

1000 B.C.
Illyrians move into Balkan Peninsula.

228 B.C.
Romans occupy the region; establish Province of Illyricum.

753 B.C.
Rome is founded.

116–17 B.C.
The Roman Empire reaches its greatest extent, under Emperor Trajan (98–17).

A.D. 600
Height of Mayan civilization

700–1800
Byzantine Empire controls the region; Cyril and Methodius convert many to Eastern Orthodox Church; create the Cyrillic alphabet.

900
Kingdom of Bosnia formed.

1000
The Chinese perfect gunpowder and begin to use it in warfare.

1100–1463
Hungarian *bans* (viceroys) govern Bosnia.

1350
Kingdom of Herzegovina is added to Bosnia; the two are never again separate states.

1463
Ottoman Turks take control of the region; many South Slavs are converted to Islam.

1530
Beginning of trans-Atlantic slave trade organized by the Portuguese in Africa

1558–1603
Reign of Elizabeth I of England

1620
Pilgrims sail the *Mayflower* to America.

1776
U.S. Declaration of Independence

1789–99
The French Revolution

1861
The U.S. Civil War begins.

1869
The Suez Canal is opened.

1875
Bosnia-Herzegovina breaks away from the Ottoman Empire.

1912–13
Balkan countries fight for their independence.

IN BOSNIA-HERZEGOVINA	IN THE WORLD
1914 Gavrilo Princip assassinates the heir to the Austro-Hungarian throne.	**1914** World War I begins.
	1939 World War II begins.
1941 German troops invade Yugoslavia. Croatian *Ustasa* kills Jews and Serbs en masse.	
1945 Postwar Yugoslavia formed; Tito and the Communists in control for 45 years.	**1945** The United States drops atomic bombs on Hiroshima and Nagasaki.
	1949 The North Atlantic Treaty Organization (NATO) is formed.
	1957 The Russians launch Sputnik.
	1966–69 The Chinese Cultural Revolution
	1986 Nuclear power disaster at Chernobyl in Ukraine
1991 Croatia, Slovenia, and Macedonia declare their independence from Yugoslavia.	**1991** Break-up of the Soviet Union
1992 Bosnia-Herzegovina declares independence; civil war erupts.	
1993 United Nations War Crimes Tribunal formed to investigate Serbian war crimes against Muslims.	
1995 Signing of Dayton (Ohio) Agreement.	
1996–2003 Bosnians begin long process of rebuilding and healing.	**1997** Hong Kong is returned to China.
	2001 Terrorists crash planes in New York, Washington, D.C., and Pennsylvania.
	2003 War in Iraq

GLOSSARY

bans (BAHNS)
Hungarian viceroys, or governors, sent to rule in the name of the Austrian-Hungarian empire, but exercised a good deal of independent control.

bezistan (BEZZ-is-stahn)
A domed building in Turkish bazaars that housed the shops of craftspeople.

Bogomilism
A Medieval religion based on the concept of the world as a struggle between good and evil; declared a heresy by the Roman Catholic Church, the sect slowly died out.

bora
Fierce winds from the north that bring bitterly cold winters to Bosnia.

cevapcici (CHAY-VAHP-chee-chee)
Sausages stuffed with ground meat and spices, served in pita bread.

Cyrillic
Alphabet created in the 9th century by 2 brothers, Saints Cyril and Methodius, to help introduce the Bible to South Slavs; still in use in Serbian Republic and several countries.

dorucak (DOE-ru-chak)
Bosnian for breakfast.

Janissary
A member of the Ottoman elite personal guard.

karst terrain
Areas of limestone outcroppings characterized by jagged depressions, caves, and sink holes; the name is now applied to similar landscapes throughout the world.

Organization for Security & Cooperation in Europe (OSCE)
Organization that works for a balance among the various ethnic/religious groups in Bosnia.

Partisans
Yugoslav resistance fighters, including Bosnians, who fought under Marshal Tito to drive out the Germans in World War II.

polje (POLE-jeh)
A narrow field where enough soft limestone has eroded to produce soil suitable for some crops or for grazing.

proteus (olm)
A cave-dwelling salamander-like creature; through centuries of living in complete darkness, it is nearly colorless and has no eyes.

South Slavs
Tribes that settled in the Balkans, including Croatians and Serbs.

Ustasa
The Croatian fascist organization established during World War II; responsible for the mass murder of many Serbs, Jews, and Gypsies.

FURTHER INFORMATION

BOOKS

Black, Eric. *Fractured Region.* World in Conflict Series. Minneapolis: Lerner Publications, 1999.

Connell, Janice T. *The Visions of the Children: The Apparitions of the Blessed Mother at Medjugorje.* New York: St. Martin's Press, 1992.

Filipovic, Zlata. *Zlata's Diary: A Child's Life in Sarajevo.* New York: Penguin Books, 1994.

Fireside, Harvey and Bryna J. Fireside. *Young People from Bosnia Talk About War.* Berkeley Heights, New Jersey: Enslow Publishers, 1996.

Flint, David. *Bosnia: Can There Ever Be Peace?* Topics in the News Series. Texas: Raintree Steck-Vaughn, 1994.

Gabrielpillai, Matilda. *Bosnia and Herzegovina.* Countries of the World Series. Milwaukee, WI: Gareth Stevens Publishing, 2001.

Greenberg, Keith Elliot. *Civil War in Europe.* Children in Crisis Series. San Diego: Blackbirch Marketing, 1995.

Silverman, Robert Landew. *A Bosnian Family.* A Journey Between Two Worlds Series. San Diego: Lucent Books, 1996.

WEBSITES

BBC News country profile. http://news.bbc.co.uk/1/hi/world/europe/country_profiles/1066886.stm

CIA World Factbook. www.cia.gov/cia/publications/factbook/geos/bk.html

News from the Bosnian Institute in London. www.bosnia.org.uk/news

Pavarotti Music Centre in Mostar. www.pavarottimusiccentre.com/mostar.html

The World Bank Group. http://web.worldbank.org

UNESCO: Mostar—Rebuilding of the Stari Most Bridge. www.unesco.org/opi2/mostar/introduction.htm

Because Internet listings change so rapidly and frequently, the best approach is to use your favorite search engine and type in "Bosnia" and a key word, like the name of a city, or a topic, such as "family life" or "food." Also, you might find it useful to put quotation marks around the search phrase, for example: "Bosnia—Family Life." Without the quotations, the search engine will list references to family and life, even though the listings have nothing to do with Bosnia.

VIDEOS

Eastern Europe, seventh edition. Lonely Planet Video, 2003.

For the Children of Bosnia. UNI/London Classics, 1996.

While America Watched—Bosnia's War. PBS Home Video, 1997.

BIBLIOGRAPHY

Grolier Editors. *Lands and People*, Vol. 4. Danbury, Connecticut: Grolier Publishing, 1993.

Kirking, Gale A. *A Search for Understanding: Untangling Bosnia and Herzegovina.* Madison, Wisconsin: A Real World Press, 1999.

Lonely Planet. *Eastern Europe.* Victoria, Australia: Lonely Planet Publications, 2003.

Malcolm, Noel. *Bosnia: A Short History.* New York: Harpers, 1996.

Marshall Cavendish. *Encyclopedia of World Geography.* vol. 13, *Eastern Europe.* Tarrytown, New York: 2002.

World Book Editors. *The World Book Encyclopedia of People and Places.* Vol. 1 Chicago: World Book, Inc., 2000.

Decade of Transition. Florence, Italy: United Nations Children's Fund/Innocenti Research Centre, 2001.

INDEX

143

DATE DUE

Bob Weinstein is also the author of:

Winning the Battle with Your Money Hang-ups

Get Strong

Your Career in Public Relations

RESUMES FOR HARD TIMES

Bob Weinstein

A FIRESIDE BOOK
Published by Simon and Schuster
NEW YORK

A Fireside Book
Published by Simon & Schuster, Inc.
Simon & Schuster Building
Rockefeller Center
1230 Avenue of the Americas
New York, New York 10020

FIRESIDE and colophon are registered trademarks of Simon & Schuster, Inc.
Designed by Levavi & Levaui
Manufactured in the United States of America
Printed and bound by Semline, Inc.
    3 4 5 6 7 8 9 10

Library of Congress Cataloging in Publication Data

Weinstein, Bob, date
    Resumes for hard times.

    "A Fireside book."
    1. Résumés (Employment)   I. Title.
HF5383.W36   1982   650.1′4   82-16742
ISBN 0-671-45826-4

ISBN 0-671-45826-4

CONTENTS

Acknowledgments

Special thanks to Mike Keough, Richard Cronin, James Conzelman, and George Nobbe for providing solid, well-substantiated information on the current job market; Lois de la Haba for first-rate, targeted advice; Jenny Weinstein for accumulating and evaluating statistical surveys; and Josh Weinstein for helping to transcribe and edit interview material.

For Bonnie

RESUMES FOR HARD TIMES

Urgent!

The smart job seeker sees himself realistically. He neither underestimates nor overestimates his talents. He knows it's a tough, competitive job market, and he knows how to capture the job he's after. He knows he has to be top notch, a winner in every sense of the word. Everything has to be working for him at the same time—the right credentials, appearance, attitude, experience. In sum, he has to have his act together.

It's a whole new ball game played by new rules. Understand from the onset that no one is waiting for you. You have to prove yourself and make your presence known.

This is not the 60s and 70s when good jobs were a lot easier to find and the competition wasn't as fierce. If you think the job market is tough now, just wait. As we rocket into the high-technology 21st century, the job market will be even tougher and more demanding than it is right now. In the 60s, you could earn a decent living with a liberal arts degree. In the future, you'll have to have a lot more working for you. With each passing year, the job market becomes more specialized and technologically based.

The present job market can be defined by one word: erratic. Inflation is still with us (and will be for some time), the unemployment rate is too high, yet there are plenty of jobs to be had. It's just a question of knowing what and where they are, and how to find them. Engineers; technicians of all kinds; medical, computer, and white-collar workers; highly skilled people in a variety of industries, to name just a few, have little trouble finding jobs. The job market is marked by stability and growth in some sectors, and uncertainty and shortages in others, rendering it more complicated than that of any other period in our history. Some industries are shutting plants and paring staffs, while others are retooling to meet new technological demands.

In the past, women accounted for a minuscule part of the labor force. Today, on average, over 52 percent of all women 16 and over are gainfully employed. For blue-collar crafts jobs alone the number of employed women more than doubled in the early 80s, compared with a 13 percent advance for men. Because of inflation and an outrageously high standard of living, women with small children and retired workers are forced to reenter the job market after a prolonged absence.

New industries are spawning new jobs. As a result, workers are shifting gears midcareer to take advantage of exciting job opportunities. In this supersonic age, it's quite common for a working couple to uproot themselves and cart kids, pets, and household paraphernalia cross country to take better jobs.

The byword today is change. The world is changing right before our eyes, and if you hope to grow and prosper, you'd best change with it or be left in its wake.

What does all this mean for the job seeker? It means she has to be razor sharp, on her toes, and in touch with the marketplace. To capture that special job, you have to have something special going for you. And it all begins with your resume. The personnel director of a large company or a prestigious head hunter doesn't have the faintest idea you are just what the doctor ordered. The challenge is to convey that fact via your resume, which is the first all-important step to capturing a good job.

Before you walk into a prospective employer's office for a preliminary interview, you have to convince him you are the quintessential job applicant. Your resume accomplishes just that. A well-structured terse resume allows you access to the corporate world. The rest is up to you. A poorly prepared resume gets you nowhere. You'll be scratching the surface, banging on doors, viewing the working world from the outside, wondering where you went wrong.

What most job-hunting and resume books fail to point out is that searching for the job of your choice is a job in itself. You can't go about it using a buckshot approach. As you'll soon see, it takes planning, thought, time, and work.

In the pages that follow, I've carefully placed the resume within the context of the current job market, and painstakingly outlined the crucial steps necessary to formulate a perfect resume that will land you the job you're after.

Grab a pencil, a stack of paper, and let's get started.

—Bob Weinstein

one

Tactics for a New Job Market

In a precarious economy like ours, you could be fired tomorrow. There you are happily selling widgets one day, and all of a sudden your sales director calls you in and reads you your last rites. Your mouth drops, the freshly poured coffee you're sipping spills all over your new pinstripe. You feel like the floor is giving way beneath your feet. You're in a momentary state of shock. You didn't see it coming. You didn't know that widget sales were declining steadily in most European markets, that three of the company's plants were about to be shut down, that production costs had gone through the roof. Management expects you to be sympathetic. But the harsh reality is you're out of a job, which means two weeks hence, after your severance pay is used up, your income stops. Chilling thought. What are you going to do? Are you going to try to get a job selling a similar product, or will you try something new? What are your career options?

Or let's say you're new to this strange new work world. You've just graduated from one of the foremost technical colleges with a degree in electrical engineering. You know there are jobs out there crying for your talents. But the puzzling question is how do you actually go about finding that special job that capitalizes on your talents?

Both of these job applicants, the experienced worker who lost his job and the recent college grad, begin their job search with their resumes. The ex-widget salesman frantically retrieves his dusty resume that he's not looked at in years from a drawer to see what can be done to whip it into shape, and our hot-to-trot shiny new engineer scratches his head and tries to figure out how he can best list his qualifications and goals on a sheet of paper so he can land a good job. Both individuals face a challenging exercise, one that requires thought, patience, skill, and planning.

I'm not going to take the easy way out and give you a pep talk about how important resumes are, followed by an all-purpose formula on how to write one. What else is new?

First, resumes have always been important. Let's go one step further and place the resume within the context of this haywire, unpredictable economy. To appreciate how important a resume is, it helps to understand the psychology of the present marketplace. Today a resume is more than important, it is *vital*. As one recruitment officer put it, "A good resume is as important as a well-tailored suit."

You probably think a resume is another tiresome bureaucratic exercise designed to make your life more complicated than it already is. Like job application blanks, civil service examinations, military medical examinations, compulsory health insurance examinations, you name it. On one level, that's true enough; writing a resume is one of life's obligatory chores. But so is working five days a week, eating three meals a day, and sleeping. Like death and taxes, writing a resume is another fact of life few of us can escape. The big difference today, however, is that what was once a distasteful chore is now a crucial step in the job-seeking process that can no longer be approached with perfunctory indifference. Think of it as swallowing castor oil, shaving, or going on a diet, giving up cigarettes or booze, and you'll wind up on the short end of the stick by not getting the job you envisioned for yourself, or worse yet, not getting any job at all. Face that fact now before you waste precious time.

We're moving at a breathtaking pace. We're trying to find good jobs that will give us everything we need, make us happy, and most important, that will be viable a few decades down the road. The workplace has changed. To say that machines are rapidly replacing people is understating the times. This is no longer the machine age. It is the high-speed high-technology information age where major breakthroughs are occurring while you read this page; where robots are working side by side with human beings; where computers turn our cities off and on, coordinating and ordering our lives without our knowing it. We're approaching the dawn of the 21st century. We're orbiting through time and space at hair-raising speeds. And we'd best be prepared to work and prosper within this new setting.

In *The Third Wave*, Alvin Toffler describes the worker of the future: "What Third Wave employers increasingly need therefore are men and women who accept responsibility, who understand how their work dovetails with that of others, who can handle even larger tasks, who adapt swiftly to changed circumstances, and who are sensitively tuned in to the people around them." Where workers in the past were supported by a few hundred dollars in machinery, today's worker is assisted by a sophisticated interlocking network of machines and computers totaling many thousands of dollars per employee.

Our work environment has changed drastically. We work fewer hours yet we produce more, and the four-day work week will, according to many industrial engineers, be a reality in the 21st century. As Toffler also outlined, work schedules will also be altered. With flextime, a method by which workers set their own work schedules to their biological and emotional rhythms, the nine-to-five work routine will be another vestige of the past. The night owls among us can work the lobster shift from six to twelve, or one to eight in the morning, while the rest of us work the traditional day shift.

Change is taking place faster than we can contemplate, and we have little choice but to make the mental adjustment or be consumed by our own technology. Our lifestyles, attitudes, and work environment have changed. To function in the new marketplace, it's important to make that adjustment as soon as possible. As I said in the introduction, getting a job today is not easy, and it's not going to get any easier as we wend our way into the next century. Before you muster your resources, know the ground rules. There is no time for self-deception, fruitless fantasizing, and idle talk. In the end, you'll only succeed in fooling yourself. Before you put on your coat and hat and slip your attache case under your arm, know what to expect and what the givens are. A few of these important givens follow.

It's a highly specialized job market. You have to have something concrete to offer in the form of a high-technology skill, aptitude, service. If you can't meet the demands of the job market, you're going to be sitting home watching soap operas until the cows come home. Either that or you'll wind up back in college or in a vocational school studying a high-demand skill such as tool-and-die making or molding, or possibly body-fender repair. That anthropology degree propped in a prominent spot on your fireplace mantel is as useless as a discarded dinner napkin.

For many occupations, the labor supply far exceeds the demand. Another gruesome eye opener all job seekers have to come to terms with. Come to your senses quickly. If you've got your sights set on a glamorous high paying job, know from the onset that there are a couple of thousand applicants hot to get their hands on the same position.

Competition is fierce. Following the above to its logical conclusion, the job market will become more competitive as the good jobs become scarcer and scarcer.

Versatility counts. And since old jobs are constantly being phased out and replaced by faster, newer production methods, you'd best be flexible, adaptable, and versatile. If you can't accept change, pack your things immediately and head for the back country. The new worker has to be ready to switch gears at a moment's notice. Just as machines have to be retooled to produce better and more efficient products, workers will be phased into new, cost-efficient production systems.

The person we're describing is the new technocrat, the new worker who is equipped and prepared to handle the pressures of the day. There are many pressures, and it's best to see them all before we help you shape a resume that is designed to meet the requirements of this tough new job market.

There it is in a nutshell. It's only fair to set the tone and paint the current job picture as it is. Now that you know what the job market is like—its demands, restrictions, pitfalls—you can appreciate how important it is to have a resume that can meet it and open the right doors. But before we go any further, let's learn something about ourselves.

two

Who Are You and What Can You Do?

Before you write the winning resume that's going to knock any personnel director clear out of his seat with wild-eyed excitement, know yourself from stem to stern. Understand from the onset that the resume must be a definitive statement about *you*. It doesn't beat around the bush. In seconds, it tells a reader all he/she wants to know.

Let's proceed logically. Before we can build the house, we have to construct the foundation. Once that is completed, we can think about buying the bricks, cement, wood, and nails.

Before you write your resume, have a crystal-clear idea what you're all about, what your talents are, and most important, where you're going and why.

Self-evaluation Test

To help you through this process, spend 20 minutes filling out the accompanying self-evaluation test.

SELF-EVALUATION TEST

1. What kind of job do you want? _____

2. Why did you choose this field? _____

3. What are your strong selling points? _____

_____

4. What do you have over other applicants? _____

_____

5. What are your weak points? _____

_____

6. If you don't get the job you're after, what is your second choice? _____

_____

7. Do you consider yourself highly marketable? _____

8. Do you have any interests, hobbies, or athletic abilities that might make you a more attractive job candidate? _____

_____

9. How would you classify your personality: introversive, extraversive, reclusive? _____

_____

10. Do you enjoy being your own boss, or do you prefer being supervised? _____

_____

11. Do you prefer working for a large or small organization? _____

12. Do you prefer working indoors or outdoors, and how do you feel about travel? _____

_____

The test is only a brief sample of the kind of questionnaire you can expect when you're out pounding the pavement, talking to personnel directors and company officials. No matter what they call it, the goal for any such questionnaire is the same. A prospective employer wants to know as much as possible about you before saying, "We'd love to have you join our company" or, "I'm sorry, but you don't fulfill all our requirements." The bottom line is, What profit-minded company isn't hungry for an employee who will make a significant contribution to profits, someone who will be delighted to have the job, someone who will give 150 percent.

Again, I can't stress enough the importance of doing as much preliminary preparation work as you can. You'll save yourself all kinds of grief later on. The more you know about yourself and the more information you have at hand, the clearer, tighter, and more defined your resume will be.

Let's examine the questions more closely.

1. What kind of a job do you want? Seems obvious enough, but you'd be surprised how many applicants are not sure of what they want to do and the kind of job they're after. You can't write a resume until your career goals are spelled out precisely. You can discuss your past employment record and elaborate on key points, but that's only part of the picture and not the most important part by far. The company representatives scanning your resume have to be convinced you are right for the job. Beyond that, they're looking for someone who will be in synchrony with the corporate machinery, someone whose goals are identical with those of the corporation. Again, busy personnel representatives sifting through hundreds, sometimes thousands of resumes at Xerox, Lockheed, IBM, INCO, etc., are not going to read every resume received. The best they can do is give each one a fast glance. Only those with catchy opening lines, interesting phrasing and construction will wind up in the stack marked "follow up." In Chapter Three we'll show you how to zero in on your career goals.

2. Why did you choose this field? You won't have to include this information in your resume, but for your own edification, have a ready answer. It helps crystallize your near- to long-term career goals. And chances are a corporate recruiter will drop this question on you. Be prepared beforehand. A clear, concise answer shows you've given your career careful thought and that a lot of mental energy has gone into career planning.

Personnel directors want people who will grow with the company and rise through the corporate ranks. They're not interested in nine-to-five clock watchers who already have their coats and hats on minutes before the workday ends.

You'll soon see how careful resume preparation helps with every step of the job-seeking process. If you're looking for an engineering job, for example, and a company representative asks why you chose the field and you answer, "It seemed like a good idea at the time," or, "I knew there was a real demand for engineers and their earning potential is fantastic," what do you think your chances are of getting that job?

Saying "It seemed like a good idea at the time" is analogous to signing your own death warrant. Go no further. No matter how brilliant and talented you are, you've been crossed off the list. You're no longer in the running.

As for the money part, yes, money is certainly important, but it's bad form to tell a corporate recruiter that you're pursuing a career for the money alone. If money is your sole motive, keep it to yourself. Saying it to the wrong person at the wrong time could jeopardize your chances of getting a job. Have a ready and intelligent answer to this question, something like, "Ever since I was a child I was fascinated by how things worked, what made clocks tick and motors run. In my early teens I constructed small engines, alarms, and even my own ham radio set. Electrical engineering gave me the opportunity to combine my mechanical abilities with electrical theory. As far back as I can remember, there was never any question about what I wanted to do with my life."

The above answer is a tad long winded, but if you were a personnel director, would you doubt for a second that this person loved his field and that he was an ideal candidate? When preparing your resume, a love and excitement for your career must filter through the lines to the reader.

3. What are your strong selling points? You say you're not in touch with them. Well, now is the time to start thinking about them if you hope to write a selling resume. You're not the only person looking for a job; you've got a lot of competition. Before you sit down and write your resume, be able to reel off five of your key selling points without batting an eyelash.

4. What do you have over other applicants? If you can separate yourself from your competition, you've got the razor's edge. Are you special because you skipped two grades in high school; or because you graduated second, or possibly first in your class; or because you were the only one who built a computer from scratch for a term project in college? Your good looks alone are not going to get you hired. Noteworthy achievements and good grades can put you yards ahead of other applicants.

5. What are your weak points? This is not something you're going to brag about in either your resume or in interviews. If you're still bedwetting at 32, keep that personal detail between you and your analyst. The point is to know yourself reasonably well—the good, bad, stable, and not-so-stable sides of your personality. Being in touch with your weak points often helps highlight your strong points.

6. If you don't get the job you're after, what is your second choice? I don't suggest that anyone settle, but it's important to be realistic about the current job market. Like any other marketplace, it is governed by the law of supply and demand, and naturally, in high demand areas, you'll always have a buyer's market. Knowing this, it's common sense to have an alternate or fallback position, just in case you don't get the job you're shooting for. Flexibility is important. What if a personnel director says you're in a runner-up spot and the company is interested in hiring you in an auxiliary position and some time in the future you'll be moved into the job you originally applied for? Be prepared for all eventualities. The above-mentioned scenario is not uncommon, and it's often an opportunity not to be passed up.

7. Do you consider yourself highly marketable? Even if you're in a tough area, go into the ring hell-bent on winning. Negative, pessimistic attitudes have a way of seeping through your pores, and recruiters are pretty good at picking up the vibrations. No matter what kind of a job you're after, see yourself as marketable and visualize yourself succeeding.

View yourself as a hot property, and think about clever ways to communicate that fact via your resume. More on that later.

8. Do you have any interests, hobbies, or athletic abilities that might make you a more attractive job candidate? This may or may not be relevant. Like large universities, many of our sprawling conglomerates sponsor their own athletic teams, and some of them are a cut above the average. Company football, soccer, and basketball teams are common. Some companies fly their superjocks all over the world in order to compete with other companies. If you were an outstanding athlete in college, mention it in your resume. You never know when your prior athletic victories might come in handy.

9. How would you classify your personality: introversive, extraversive, reclusive? If you plan on working in a research think tank, buried under a microscope, it doesn't matter what kind of personality you have. But if you plan on making a splash in the corporate world, you'd better be good with people. Another important point that should ooze through your resume verbiage.

10. Do you enjoy being your own boss, or do you prefer being supervised? We all work differently. Some of us prefer a group setting, supervised by one or a number of people, while others prefer being put in a corner so they can get their work done at their own pace. Where do you fit in? If you fall into the self-starter category, for instance, highlight it in your resume. Corporate recruiters can't get enough take-charge self-starter types. They're considered triple-A-rated job candidates.

11. Do you prefer working for a large or small organization? Some of us prefer being big cogs in small wheels, while others enjoy being small cogs in oversized wheels. Which are you? Not all of us will enjoy working in the corporate headquarters of a major conglomerate the likes of Gulf & Western or IT&T. You might need a smaller, regional-type company. Before you plan your job-hunting strategy, try to place yourself within the corporate machinery. Even if things don't work out as planned, carve a niche for yourself and work towards it.

12. Do you prefer working indoors or outdoors, and how do you feel about travel? Not everyone wants to be buried behind a desk all day long. Account executives employed by public relations firms and advertising agencies divide their time between field and office work. Salespeople thrive on spending 50 percent or more of their time on the road visiting clients and rustling up new business. It's important to make these preferences known, either via a resume or interview. Some jobs involve no travel, others 10 percent travel, all the way up to 75 percent of your time on the road.

When you've completed the self-evaluation test, study your answers. Aside from getting to know yourself a little better, use the questionnaire to compare yourself with other job seekers, real or imaginary. Give the questionnaire to friends or family, and see how your answers compare with theirs. The information will be valuable in putting together your resume.

Checking Out the Terrain

Once you know a little bit more about yourself, study the marketplace. Don't go off half-cocked. Ask yourself the following questions.

- Where are the jobs in my field?
- What companies dominate the field?
- Are they large multinational companies with divisions all over the world, or is my industry populated by small family-owned companies scattered about a particular region?
- If most of the jobs are confined to another part of the country, am I willing to relocate? Can I make a satisfactory adjustment?

It all boils down to research and fact gathering. You're moving right along now. There is no question about what you want to do and where your greatest potential lies. Now the trick is mapping out a realistic course of action, or battle plan.

I don't know about you, but I'm somewhat of a nut when it comes to creating systems for myself. Through trial and error, I've discovered that a well-constructed system is just about foolproof. First, there is security knowing you're covering your field logically, and second, it's the fastest way to get things done. There is no guesswork, and no puzzled grimaces at the end of the day, wondering if you did everything you were supposed to do.

The system you use is up to you. A systems analyst friend, for instance, with 12 years of experience behind him, decided it was time to move to a better, higher-paying job. To get a clear picture of where the jobs in his field were, he bought a chart-size map (the kind military planners use) and pinned it to a wall in his home office. One rainy Saturday, with the help of a felt-tipped pen, he put all the major computer companies in their appropriate places on the map. Three hours later he proudly stepped a few feet from his map and, feeling like a conquering general, scanned the map, secure in knowing he had an unobstructed overview of the jobs in his industry. He wasn't finished. Next, he starred the companies he'd like to work for and considered the possibilities of relocating to different parts of the country. No small decision.

That's one way to proceed. Other strategy-minded job applicants set up control charts to log material in and out and carefully track correspondence to and from companies. (More on systems and logs in later chapters.)

You say you don't have time to fool with charts, maps, and logging correspondence in and out. Before closing the door on that suggestion, think about it for a while. As much as you want to move to the front lines to see what's out there, exercise some restraint. You won't regret it later on. By getting the lay of the land, and precisely determining where your best opportunities lie, you're reducing the chance of error. By weighing the pros and cons of a job strategy, you're also studying your competition. And the competition is not to be underestimated for a millisecond.

In the end, the thoughtful job logician wins. If at the end of the road is a superior job with excellent growth potential, a week, two weeks, even a month of painstaking research is worth the effort.

See the world as it is, not as you'd like to see it. Dreaming about a good job is fun, but it doesn't put a farthing in your pocket. In the final analysis, the pragmatist scores. To make inroads in this tricky job market, tactics are called for. The smart job seeker is aware of this from the beginning and plans his strategy accordingly. Think like a general, not a foot soldier.

three

Playing the Resume Game

Ready to get down to brass tacks? You know what you want and you know what the market is like. Now let's gather our forces and go after that special job. Let's look at the resume, find out what it does, why it's important, and how it can open that heavy creaking door into your future.

It's time to play the resume game. Why a game? Because it is, and if you see it as such, you'll approach the job market with the same controlled, competitive spirit a football player demonstrates as he ambles onto the playing field, or that of a boxer walking to his corner, ready to destroy his opponent as soon as the bell rings.

A game, whether it's on the playing field or between rival businesses, is a serious pursuit. There are many definitions for the word. My favorites, taken right from *Webster's New Collegiate Dictionary*, are "A procedure or strategy for gaining an end; tactic" or "A field of gainful activity."

In *The Money Game*, Adam Smith writes, "If you are a player in the Game, or are thinking of becoming one, there is one irony of which you should be aware. The object of the game is to make money, hopefully a lot of it." In *Power*, Michael Korda writes, "All life is a game of power. The object of the game is simple enough: to know what you want and get it."

And the object of the resume game is to write a perfect resume that will get you the job you want. Not any job, but the one you *really want*.

Now let's take a closer look at the resume.

What It Is Not

A resume is not:

- Your life story typed neatly on two pieces of letter-size paper
- A chronological listing of dates and places
- A boring recount of your life to the present
- An exercise in tedium
- A compilation of self-congratulatory adjectives

In other words, it can't be whipped together the way a short-order cook knocks out bacon and eggs and home fries, with dazzling speed and dash. Or as one cynical personnel director put it, "A resume can't be a snow job. We're getting pretty damned good at weeding them out and tossing them in the wastebasket."

What Is a Resume?

A resume is simply a brief, well-documented account of your career qualifications. That's an adequate description, but it doesn't tell the whole story. Better yet, a resume is a capsulized account that *highlights* and describes *significant* aspects of your background and qualifications for a given job.

A resume is many different things. It is a statement of purpose, a summation. Realistically, it is a sales promotion tool designed to sell you. The key words are *tool* and *sell*. Just as a knife is a sharp metal device used to cut things, a chair is a seat traditionally having four legs and a back, a resume's purpose is to sell you.

Simple? So why do millions of us expend unnecessary words turning out resumes that are wordy, pointless, and unfocused. Answer: We don't deem the effort important. Hence, the product is sloppy, ineffectual, and if you're lucky, it might get you an interview. But luck doesn't count for too much in this job market.

As I said in Chapter One, writing a resume for most of us can be likened to taking medicine. Don't think about it; just do it and get it over with. Unlike taking medicine, producing a quickie resume will make you feel better for the moment. But the anxiety and frustration come when your slapdash resume gets you nowhere.

What is a resume? To be even more accurate, it is your personal advertisement. The challenge is producing one that works, one that sells you to an employer, one that gets you interviews. It's easy producing a resume. You can probably write one in less than an hour. But I wouldn't put any money on that resume. Turning out a winning, superior resume is another matter altogether. It's impossible to say how long it takes to turn out a quality resume. One person might put four or five hours into the effort, while someone else requires a couple of days to gather thoughts so everything fits together in a logical order.

In the long run the time factor isn't the all-important question. What is important is writing a resume that accomplishes its goal. The amount of words used in an average resume can range from 250 to 600 plus. Not very many words to sum up your life, demonstrate you're highly motivated, qualified, and the right person for the job.

Look at it another way. What if we dispensed with resumes altogether? Before you applaud, think about it for a moment. Place yourself within the context of the present job market. There you are, along with millions of other qualified applicants hot to get your hands on the right job. Or if desperate, any job. If we dispensed with resumes, we'd have no choice but to go to the next phase of the recruitment process—the interview. The average interview takes about 45 minutes, and some as long as an hour and a half. If every applicant had to be interviewed, how many applicants would be hired in a given day, week, month, or year? The answer is not very many. And translated in terms of you, the job seeker, it points to a dismal situation indeed. You might have little choice but to apply for welfare until your turn in the interview process comes along. And we haven't even gotten to the hiring process.

Need I go further? If there were no resumes, few people, regardless of the industry, would be hired each year. The unemployment rate would be staggering, and there would be millions of unhappy people roaming the streets.

Why a Resume?

A resume is a time saver. It not only saves employers', recruiters', and placement managers' time, it saves you time as well. Think about that before you rant and scream at the thought of preparing your first resume, or rewriting your old one.

Be practical. The 90s are just around the corner, and forward-thinking industrialists are already tooling up for the 21st century. Time is of the essence. We know we can produce just about anything quickly and efficiently. We pride ourselves on being precise, accurate, and functional. This is an age of super specialization and high technology, where engineers and technicians are more valuable than anthropologists, zoologists, paleontologists, and philosophers. The emphasis is on purpose and function. The more functional you are, the more valuable you are. In these hard times you don't hear too many college students saying, "I don't know what I'm going to do with my life" or, "I think I'll take a year or two off so I can get my head together before settling into a career." Not unless they have a sizable trust fund sitting in a savings bank somewhere.

What with rocketing college costs, I'd say that nine out of ten college freshmen know exactly what they want in life and how to get it.

The irony, according to Mike R. Keough, vice president and general manager of the New York–based executive search firm ExecuSearch, is that we train people for skills, trades, and professions, yet we don't show them the techniques necessary to get those jobs. It's a rough job market, he contends, "but there are jobs out there. You just have to know how to find them."

Who Needs One?

Today, practically everyone needs a job. "A good resume is vital, unless you're so prominent and well known that your reputation and credentials precede you," says James Conzelman, executive director of the Association of Executive Recruiting Consultants, Inc. If you're a high-ranking executive who has shuttled between major corporations and is practically a household word in corporate circles, resumes are seldom seen or mentioned. Prestige job offers are often discussed and confirmed on the golf course, over drinks at expensive restaurants, or flying first class 30,000 feet above the clouds. Don't concern yourself with this elite class of corporate superstars. Their earnings are way above the national average, and they account for a tiny percentage of the work force.

Highly skilled craftspeople can also move from job to job without resumes. Seasoned tool-and-die makers, machinists, electricians, mold makers, for example, don't always have to prepare a resume when changing jobs. They move within restricted circles of highly skilled craftspeople, and their reputations usually precede them. Many employers insist that word of mouth is the most effective way to hire skilled workers. A resume only presents one aspect of a worker's skill potential. But a five-minute conversation with an applicant's prior shop foreman tells a prospective employer all he needs to know.

The rest of us, however, are not that fortunate. The two job minorities—the elite executive class and the skilled craftsperson—are at opposite ends of the job spectrum. The rest of us fall into the middle and have to play the game according to the rules. And the game plan calls for a resume.

Positive Attitude

The place to start is with the right attitude. Before you put pen to paper, prepare yourself for the event. By now you know a resume can't be whipped together in a few hours. Resume writing may never be fun, yet you're one step ahead of everyone else if you start with a positive attitude. Start by saying to yourself, "I'll do everything I can to turn out an excellent resume. Time is not important. My goal is to produce a winning product that will land me an excellent job." Stop. Start from that point and you're beginning on the right foot in the right rhythm.

A positive attitude focuses you on your goal and prepares you for all eventualities.

First Base Theory

A positive attitude leads to what I call the First Base Theory. At the very beginning of the job-hunting process, see yourself realistically. A resume is not going to get you a job. But it will propel you in the right direction, into the industry or company you want to work for, and get you an interview. If your resume is good, you will have the equivalent of a well-placed ball into center field, putting you on first base. Hence, the First Base

Theory. And if it's excellent or superior, you might find yourself on second base.

Suffice it to say, a good resume puts you securely in the game. The rest is up to you. Once you're on the playing field, you have to maneuver yourself accordingly so you can move strategically from base to base, finally leaping to home plate and the job you worked so hard for. Understand from the start that you're never going to feel first base under your feet unless you have a winning resume. One job analyst estimated that in an average job market, the typical Fortune 500 company receives over 300,000 unsolicited resumes a year. But as I said, this is not a typical job market. It is a volatile and unpredictable market in the midst of an uncertain economic climate. So it's safe to assume the above figure is now a lot higher, another factor to keep in mind before tackling the current market.

Start warming up right now and understand from the onset that you've got to be good to make the major leagues. Only the pros go the distance.

Now let's find out what personnel directors are looking for.

four

What Are Personnel Directors Looking For?

Corporate recruiters and personnel directors are busy people. They don't have time to wade through chatty, rambling resumes that have to be read twice before they're understood. Richard Cronin, president of the Chicago-based executive search firm Hodge, Cronin and Associates, Inc., says his company receives an average of 400 to 500 resumes a week, more than twice the amount received a couple of years ago. That's a lot of resumes to read. But of those 500 resumes, how many will wind up on personnel directors' desks? "Only 10 percent are worth retaining," sighs Cronin. "Most of the resumes we receive are horrible. We read all of them. The problem is determining whether we want to retain them in our active file."

According to many corporate recruiters, the problem with the majority of resumes received is that they're poorly defined and lack a clear objective. As the Association of Executive Recruiting Consultants' James Conzelman puts it, "You must come to an employer clearly defined and fill a need."

As job hunter, you have to fit into someone else's system. Just as you have your own job-hunting systems and procedures, recruitment firms and employers also have systems, massive systems to be exact, with codes and numbers that can be put into and pulled out of computers by flicking a switch.

If your resume touches a responsive chord, you will be put into the system. If it doesn't, you'll wind up in someone's file, or worse yet, in a wastepaper basket.

Most recruitment firms code their applicants according to function. That way they can service their clients more efficiently. If the International Widget Company, for instance, is looking for a top financial person to head their quality control unit, the executive search firm commissioned to fill the job will process the detailed job description under the heading "financial management," with a possible subheading, "quality control experience." Hence, the need for clarity. "If we can't code a resume, we can't put it into our retrieval system," explains Cronin.

Targeting Your Resume

Regardless of your field, your resume must be targeted to a specific job. From the onset, your goal is to write a resume that goes right into the corporate hopper.

"If people don't know where they are going, they will wind up someplace else," asserts Mike Keough of ExecuSearch. "I guarantee it. They're going to be unhappy, unemployed, and worse yet, they're going to be unplaceable. The problem with a lot of people looking for jobs today is they don't know precisely what they do for a living. They don't have a grasp of their jobs, and they don't understand their own industries. The first thing you have to do before you write your resume is think about what you want to do with your life. If you don't have a clear career objective, you'd better think one up."

Career Direction

A job amounts to a nine-to-five routine, culminating in a paycheck at the end of the week. A career, on the other hand, is a lifetime pursuit that extends beyond the narrowly defined limits of a nine-to-five job.

Personnel directors are not so much interested in job hunters as they are career builders. The former have their sights set on short-term goals, the latter have a global plan with well-defined goals.

The smart job seeker sees his career outlined in orderly time frames, which break out into short-term, intermediate-term, and finally long-term goals. His immediate goal is not so much to earn $100,000 a year, but more practically, to create a master plan consisting of a number of stepping-stone jobs leading to that $100,000 salary.

You don't have to be a brilliant job candidate to list a logical career objective that shows you're building a career for yourself. Before you can convince a personnel director you know what you want, it helps if you clearly see your career path. Before you construct your resume, start thinking along logical career lines. Can a baby run before he or she walks or crawls? Can you practice law without a law degree, perform an appendectomy without a medical degree? You can try, but you're not going to get very far.

Defining Your Goals

Maybe your career goals cannot be summarized neatly in three or four words. Your field may not be that clear cut. To get your career objective across, you may have to outline your route more precisely. One way to do it is to establish a goal plan which can be anything from an elaborate chart, circle, or horizontal goal path. Whatever method you use, start off with an ultimate career objective and then outline the steps necessary to reach it.

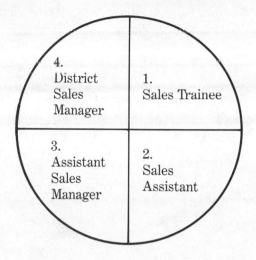

Sales Trainee	Sales Assistant	Assistant Sales Manager	District Sales Manager
1.	2.	3.	4.

Refer to the circular and horizontal plans illustrating the goal of district sales manager. Your goal chart might be a lot more complicated than these examples. It might involve an eight- or fifteen-stage process before you reach your goal, with some modifications along the way. However many stages exist along your goal path, know what they are before preparing your resume. Your resume objective is the leitmotiv for what follows. It sets the tone, creates the mood, establishes the setting. Create the wrong mood and setting by starting off in the wrong key and you'll have a disjointed, poorly constructed resume.

The Multinational Corporation

Business is not transacted the way it was a century ago. The small entrepreneur will soon be a vestige of a primitive and inoperative business environment. Today's business is conducted on a bigger and constantly expanding scale. The small family-held corporation is giving way to the publicly held multidivision corporation, which will be replaced by the larger conglomerate and the gargantuan multinational corporate entity with divisions throughout the world.

As business entities become larger and more diffuse, it's easy to get lost within the nooks and crannies of an expanding corporate machine. Get used to the idea that *small* is a nonfunctional word in today's business environment, and *big* is not as accurate as *expanding*, *multidivisional*, *multinational*. Understand the terminology and know how you fit into it.

Not all of us will be company presidents, department heads, division heads, or regional managers. Nevertheless, if we are to function effectively within the new corporate environment, it helps to see our roles precisely without our organizations. Once you've established an identity for yourself, know your career route, envision it clearly, separate yourself from your peers.

five

Constructing Your Resume

It's time to rev up the creative wheels and gather all the materials to write your resume. Just as a painter needs oils, brushes, and canvas to paint a portrait or landscape, you have to amass the bits and pieces of information needed to make your resume stand out.

What Goes In

All resumes contain the same kinds of information. Yet, there is plenty of room for variation. Mold the resume to your own situation. Soon enough, you'll see what's important, irrelevant, and of no value to a personnel representative. Your resume should include the following:

1. Vital statistics. No matter what kind of job you're after, your resume begins with your vital statistics. Name, address (include zip code), and telephone number (include area code). If currently employed, don't list your work number. Why look for trouble? It's poor form, and you run the risk of mistakenly being called by a recruitment officer at work. Beyond the embarrassment, you could wind up leaving your current job a lot sooner than planned. A diplomatic way to handle the situation is to spell out what your job situation is like in a cover letter and suggest appropriate times to call. Or simply suggest that you be called after seven in the evening at home.

2. Objective. Keep your objective short, sweet, and to the point. Some applicants feel compelled to devote paragraphs to their objective. If you can't sum up the kind of job you're looking for in several words or a couple of terse, well-constructed sentences, you're wasting your time. Like the lead in a good news story, your career objective has to hook the reader immediately. If it's too long, ambiguous, wordy, pretentious, rambling, your reader won't go any further. If the objective is unclear, the rest of the resume will be unclear. How important is the objective? Suffice it to say the entire resume revolves around it.

Must the resume have a job objective? Most resumes need one, while a tiny minority do not. There is no foolproof method for getting a job. The resume formats developed thus far have worked for the majority of job applicants. But that doesn't mean there isn't room for variation when called for.

What if you are multidimensional, with expertise in a number of areas, and you don't want to pigeonhole yourself to a specific job objective? You may have several. Many public relations, advertising, and broadcasting workers have, in the course of their careers, become proficient in a number of areas. A public relations generalist, for instance, may be a crackerjack speech writer and also a first-rate account executive. An advertising copywriter may have a similar background, excelling in both the account executive (selling) aspect of the business and the creative end as well. Broadcasting (TV and radio) workers may be competent reporters, editors, and broadcasters.

No one says you have to limit yourself to one tightly knit job function for the rest of your working life. Senior executives who have a broad-based financial background have a number of career options open to them. Within a large corporation they can work in several departments: financial planning, budget development, portfolio management, supervising accounting functions, etc.

Multifaceted applicants have a challenging job ahead of them. Like anyone else applying for a job, they also have to structure their resumes so they present a unified picture. Job recruiters are not interested in applicants who are all over the place, having dabbled in a number of fields. That points to instability, making your job-seeking efforts all the more tenuous.

One solution is to create two and possibly three resumes, covering each area of expertise. Another possibility is to write one all-purpose resume without an objective and use the cover letter as a means of honing in on the job you're after. Multiple resumes will be covered in greater detail in Chapter Thirteen. For now, know that you have leeway and can vary your resume format. The cover letter, which will also be discussed later on, can be used to replace the resume objective. Whatever format you use, your goal is to present yourself as a job applicant who knows what he/she wants and is clear about goals, objectives, and talents.

3. Business experience. The reader knows where you're headed, and now is curious to see if you have the background to match. Starting with your most recent position held, number of years worked, and title, work backwards, relating important details about each job held. This is the meat and potatoes of your resume, so think in brief, telegraph-type sentences.

Think carefully about what you did on your last job. What exactly were your responsibilities? Did you have an important position? Or, if you were an insignificant cog in a large wheel, how do you summarize your job experience so you seem more important and still keep the resume believable? What changes, if any, did you make while working for the company? How did it affect the functioning of the company? Was there a significant increase in sales and revenues?

4. Education. Your education is important, but don't go overboard listing every award, honor, and citation received since you started school. Keep it pertinent. If you were graduated from college, start with your college education. If you just have a high school diploma, mention the type of diploma you received (academic, commercial, vocational) and any special skills learned that relate to the job you are seeking. Mention grades if you were an outstanding student—straight A or high B average. Also include the year you graduated or completed training or courses.

5. Extracurricular activities. If you're fresh out of college with no work experience to speak of, it's a good idea to list relevant extracurricular activities that relate to the field you're trying to break in to. Just don't go overboard. If you are applying for a job as a chemical engineer, a job recruiter is not interested in your membership in the soccer or bible club. But if you were a good-standing member of the school engineering society, mention it. Don't clutter your resume with irrelevant information.

6. Languages. If you speak a foreign language, or possibly a few, it never hurts to mention it. You never know when a knowledge of French, Spanish, or Italian will come in handy. A company might be looking for someone to work at a foreign subsidiary. Since you are fluent in the language, you may be the ideal candidate for the job.

Optional Headings

That's it for the most important items that go into your resume. However, there are other subcategories that can also be listed, if relevant. A few to consider are:

Awards, honors, published material. If you hold some distinguished honors in your field, or an article of yours was published in the industry's trade journal, by all means mention it. It can work in your favor. You're telling the reader you are a cut above average. You are demonstrating a total commitment to your career. Or, if you were a star athlete or got into college on an athletic scholarship, mention it. You never know when it may come in handy. As we said in Chapter Two, many large companies like to have superjocks on the payroll.

Community service. So what if you headed the fund-raising section of your local church or synagogue or you're a cub scout group leader.

Congratulations. You're a nice person. But what does that have to do with the job you're applying for? Again, only if you can find a connection to the job in question, list it.

Military service. Another optional section. Depending on the length of service, your responsibilities, and its connection to the position you're applying for, it can be valuable information. If you're a nuclear technician, for example, who was trained in the navy, it should be highlighted in this section. If you are a Vietnam, Korean, or World War II veteran with a distinguished record, mention it in the space of a couple of lines. Don't overplay it. Just state the facts. War veterans hold a special status.

Marital status. You don't have to mention whether you're married, single, divorced, or if you have children or not. As a rule, employers are curious to know something about an employee's personal life. It's up to you. Some employers interpret wife, kids, and house as symbols of stability. If you mention your marital status, list it under the umbrella heading "Personal."

What Doesn't Go In

You'd be surprised what some people put into their resumes. The rule of thumb is if it's not relevant or appropriate, leave it out. Below are a list of items that don't belong in your resume.

Date. Above vital statistics, some applicants put in a date. Leave it out. The idea is to keep your resume current for as long as possible.

Physical description, health status, etc. Some applicants go to town with this section. Omit your height, weight, color of your eyes, photograph, and your health status. Who cares? You're not applying for a job as a Hollywood stuntperson (at least most of us aren't), and your physical statistics have no bearing on how well you'll do your job. In fact, it can either work for you or against you. Either way, it's serving the wrong purpose. If you're 5′3″ with blue eyes, weigh 110 pounds, and have a sunny disposition, do you want to be hired for your good looks or because you fulfill the requirements of the job?

Don't mention anything about your health either. Whether you're in top physical condition or a short step away from cardiac arrest, leave it out of your resume. The same goes for mentioning race, religion, and political affiliation.

Salary requirements. Salary is a highly sensitive subject that does not belong in a resume. Not only is it inappropriate to include either your past, present, or desired salary, but it could work against you. When an employer discusses salary, chances are you're being considered for the job. How seriously may have a lot to do with the salary you're asking for. By including a salary figure, you may either be underpricing or overpricing yourself. Your credentials may be perfect, but your salary requirements too high, knocking you out of the race without a fighting chance. Salary negotiation is an art in itself. It's to your advantage to negotiate salary on a one-to-one basis with a prospective employer. Even if you're asking for too much money, if an employer wants you badly enough, a common ground can be reached. But again, this is a matter to be discussed in the privacy of an office, or possibly over a drink after work.

Availability. If you're not available right now, don't send out your resume. If you're just fishing to see what's out there, save your time, money, and energy, and don't waste a personnel worker's time. This is a highly competitive job market, and employers are looking for qualified people who can start immediately. Nothing has to be said regarding your availability. If you are sending out your resume, an employer doesn't have to be reminded that you're ready and willing to start at once.

References. Some resumes list a number of professional and personal references, while others use the tag line "References furnished upon request" at the bottom of the resume. Omit both. This is another sensitive matter that should be discussed on a one-to-one basis with an employer. Saying you'll furnish references is a redundancy. Of course you'll give references. If IBM or Xerox is interested in you, are you going to refuse to give appropriate references? Listing two or three all-purpose references is unprofessional. A more appropriate strategy is to tailor the references to the job you're seeking.

Age. In the past you were expected to list your age on your resume. It was a great way for employers to weed out employees who were either too young or too old. If you were over 40, many employers considered you over the hill and not worth considering. According to the Age Discrimination and Employment Act of 1967 (amended in 1978), it's against the law to discriminate because of age. For the majority of jobs, age has no bearing on competence.

Reasons for leaving last job. This is an important topic, but it doesn't belong in your resume. By listing reasons for leaving your last job you may, without realizing it, jeopardize your chances of being considered for the position you're applying for. Everyone changes jobs for different reasons. Whatever the reasons, it's politic not to get into this sticky topic in your resume. The proper place is the interview, at a strategic point when a prospective employer is interested in you.

Abbreviations. Some of us opt to take the easy way out and abbreviate instead of writing out a term or word. The resume is the wrong place to abbreviate. First, it looks sloppy and unprofessional, and secondly, if they are technical abbreviations, your reader might not understand what you're talking about. However, it's perfectly okay to abbreviate degrees (B.A., B.S.), states, streets or avenues, and company and incorporated.

Now that we know what to put into and what to leave out of our resume, let's gather it all together and set up a resume worksheet.

six

How to Use a Resume Worksheet

Before we write the perfect resume, all the essential facts, details, and pertinent statistics have to be gathered. It's easier to write a clean, crisp resume if you have everything right in front of you. The resume worksheet eliminates gnawing feelings of anxiety many of us experience when we have to sit down and rake up details from our past. The advantage of the worksheet is that everything you need is at hand.

Creating a worksheet can be compared to preparing a complicated gourmet dish with many ingredients. There are two ways to proceed: the easy way and the haphazard way. In our frenzy to get the show on the road, we often opt for the haphazard approach and start to cook before we have all the ingredients. That's a risky way to proceed because we're assuming all the ingredients are in our cupboards. It never occurs to us that we might be missing a few things. Result: confusion. Just as we're drooling to get this spectacular concoction sizzling in our pans, we have to stop *in medias res* and run to the supermarket.

All that confusion could have been avoided if we simply made a list of the things we needed and then placed each item before us. Then, if we discovered we were missing something, we'd go out and buy it. These few preparatory steps could have made our jobs a lot easier.

Lesson learned: Don't put the cart before the horse. Or, it pays to be organized. The same rationale applies to writing your resume. Don't begin to write your resume unless you have all the facts in front of you. Hence, the need for a resume worksheet. Now let's set one up and fill it with the appropriate data.

To summarize, a worksheet is necessary because it:

1. Makes resume writing easy

2. Reduces chance of error

3. Provides opportunity to add pertinent information you might have forgotten

4. Encourages orderly, logical thinking

More Is Better Than Less

The worksheet is a convenient vehicle for gathering pertinent data into a logical format. The philosophy behind the worksheet is that more is better than less. Start with a great deal of information and then decide what to keep and what to drop. Don't expect to fill in every category of the worksheet. Some items won't apply to you. One applicant may have five saleable skills, another may have one, possibly two skills worth highlighting. That doesn't necessarily make the applicant with five skills more marketable. It depends upon what the demand is for the particular skill.

Many of us are more talented than we realize. So don't be ashamed to toot your own horn and list all your qualifications, talents, and skills. In listing your primary and secondary skills, you'll probably uncover skills and abilities you've forgotten about or possibly thought were unimportant. Yet to employers, your combination of skills and talents makes you all the more attractive.

In the pages that follow, you'll find a blank resume worksheet and two sample worksheets. Study the samples, then try to fill in the blank worksheet for yourself. If it doesn't meet your particular needs, alter it accordingly. You can even design your own if you wish. All you have to do is establish a workable format and fill in the appropriate spaces. You may want to use the job description questionnaire to help you in composing your job descriptions.

RESUME WORKSHEET

Name _____

_____

Address _____

_____

Telephone _____

Objectives

a. _____

_____

b. _____

_____

c. _____

_____

d. _____

_____

Summary Experience

_____

_____

_____

_____

Work History (List most recent jobs first and decide on appropriate time period to cover.)

Date started _____   Company & address

_____

Date terminated _____ - _____

Job description _____

_____

_____

Date started _____   Company & address

Date terminated _____   _____

Job description _____

_____

_____

_____

Date started _____   Company & address

Date terminated _____   _____

Job description _____

_____

_____

_____

Education

High school _____

College _____

Degree _____

Special studies _____

Languages _____

_____

Military Service _____

_____

Professional Affiliations _____

_____

Personal _____

_____

SKILLS INVENTORY CHART

Primary Skills

a. _____

_____

b. _____

_____

c. _____

_____

d. _____

_____

Secondary Skills

a. _____

_____

b. _____

_____

c. _____

_____

d. _____

_____

Backup/support Skills

a. _____

_____

b. _____

_____

c. _____

_____

JOB DESCRIPTION QUESTIONNAIRE

1. What did you do when you started your job? _____

_____

2. Outline the progression of events as you advanced in your job. _____

_____

_____

3. What skills did you bring to the job? _____

_____

4. What skills did you learn while working on the job? _____

_____

5. Did your presence have any effect on output? Describe in detail. _____

_____

6. Did you increase sales? How much and over what period of time? _____

_____

7. What was your relationship to the other employees and management? _____

_____

8. How valuable were you to the organization? _____

_____

RESUME WORKSHEET

Name   *Joan Jordon* _____

Address   *3245 Wilshire St., Boca Raton, Florida 33432* _____

_____

Telephone   *(305) 576 - 8790* _____

Objectives

a. *Work in executive capacity for major dress company*

b. *Design and create new dresses*

c. *Plan sales strategies*

d. *Supervise sales staff*

Summary Experience

Over past decade, concentrated on honing my expertise on several fronts: designing, selling, coordination, and administration. Looking for position that will challenge me on all of the above fronts.

Work History

Date started *January 1974*

Date terminated *February 1982*

Company & address *Drexel Dress Ltd., 9808 Logan Ave., Boca Raton, Florida*

Job description *Responsible for creating and designing new dresses in junior sizes for major department stores and retail outlets throughout the United States. Execute all facets of dress design from studying market, design concept, and materials to cutting fabric and supervising production of garment. Supervise staff of 25 workers. Fully responsible for meeting production schedule.*

Education

High School *Hackensack High School, Hackensack, New Jersey*

College *Cornell University, 1963-1967*

Degree *B.A. Fine Arts*

Special studies *Enrolled in special design workshop and conducted intercollegiate design forum*

Languages *Fluent in Spanish and German*

Military Service

Professional Affiliations

Personal *Married / three children*

SKILLS INVENTORY CHART

Primary Skills

a. *Design*

b. *Supervise*

c. *Long-range planning*

d. *Forecast trends*

Secondary Skills

a. *Familiar with office operations*

b. *Bookkeeping functions*

c.

d.

Backup/support Skills

a. _____

b. _____

c. _____

d. _____

RESUME WORKSHEET

Name _Louis Batchet_

Address _567 Lake Shore Rd., North Mansfield,_

Ohio 44901

Telephone _(419) 998-6442_

Objectives

a. _Work for growing mass-production company as methods engineer_

b. _Supervise, manage, and be responsible for technical and engineering phases of operation_

c. _Eventually work into upper-echelon management position_

Summary Experience

Carefully tracked my career so that I've acted as a functional intermediary between management, line engineers, and skilled workers, thus perfecting both my technical and managerial skills as a methods engineer intent on moving up the career ladder. An efficient methods engineer not only has to know how to design equipment, but maintain and run it as well.

Work History

Date started _March 1972_

Date terminated _December 1982_

Company & address
Townsend Electronics Corp., 234 Conn. Turnpike, West Hartford, Connecticut

Job description _Company manufactures and distributes industrial valves for chemical industry, has 900 employees, and four plants. Grosses $20 million annually. Began as assistant engineer, and within a year's time was promoted to associate engineer with line authority over a number of phases of quality control division. Over the years have mastered several manufacturing processes and in final year had staff of 12 engineers under me. Designed and supervised a time study program on a few of the company's major operations, thus increasing plant efficiency by 55 percent over a seven-year period. Overall, responsible for increased production capacity and increased sales by 35 percent._

Education

High School _South High, Columbus, Ohio_

College _Massachusetts Institute of Technology, 1967-1971_

Degree _Bachelor of Science, Graduated with high B average; honor student for three out of my four college years_

Special studies _Unlike most engineering students, majored in both industrial and electrical engineering_

Languages _____

Military Service _1965-1967, U.S. Army, honorable discharge, rank of master sergeant_

Professional Affiliations _Active in Engineering Society of America: served in different capacities, treasurer, and now as acting chairman_

Personal _Single_ _____

_____

SKILLS INVENTORY CHART

Primary Skills

a. _Design_ _____

b. _Construction_ _____

c. _Create improved systems_ _____

d. _____

Secondary Skills

a. _Work well with people_ _____

b. _Run large department_ _____

c. _Can fill in on plant operations_ _____

d. _Can take over some of the building functions_ _____

Backup/Support Skills

a. _Type_ _____

b. _Use word processor_ _____

c. _Familiar with office operations_ _____

d. _____

Stress Skills

Multiskilled applicants should spend time on the skills inventory chart of their worksheet. Just as the engineer in the sample worksheet listed primary, secondary, and support skills, I bet you can list some secondary and backup skills as well. Think about it.

Let's say you worked as a line supervisor in an automotive plant for the past 20 years. The plant closed down and you, along with 1,200 other automotive workers, are out of work. To make matters worse, it's not just your plant that is shutting down—the entire auto industry is in the throes of a major slump. What are your options? Do you comb the country trying to find a similar assembly line job, or do you take stock of your resources and try to find a different job utilizing your other talents. In these hard times, I suggest the latter course of action. It's a mature, practical, and feasible alternative, especially if you have a number of marketable skills.

Our line supervisor may not be able to find another assembly line job for some time, but there are other things he can do that also pay a decent salary. By filling out the skills inventory chart, he discovers talents he's forgotten about. He's also a crackerjack auto mechanic who can practically build a car from scratch. His auto skills are impressive. He can fix engines and do body repair work as well.

Taking stock of his job prospects capitalizing on his primary and secondary skills, the job outlook no longer appears so bleak. He should be able to secure work in either a replacement parts shop, auto repair shop, or possibly a body and fender shop. By stimulating the creative wheels, new job options open before his eyes. What seemed like a hopeless situation turns about, and new light appears on the horizon. (More on this in Resume Alternative Letter section of Chapter Eight.)

There are many other examples. Someone applying for an entry-level job in a junior executive training program, for instance, increases her chances of securing a job if she presents a complete picture of her skills. Especially in an executive capacity, employers prefer candidates who can do several things well. The narrowly defined job applicant is of minor interest. But the applicant with technical, supervisory, and administrative skills, for example, will ultimately be a coveted cog within a growing company.

Take your time filling out your worksheet. It's an important step in the process of preparing a selling resume. Put a little extra effort into the worksheet and you'll be delighted with the results.

seven

Writing Your Resume

Enough groundwork, now let's write that superior resume. We'll back into this topic by starting with a number of resume no-nos that can destroy your chance of ever getting an interview. From the negative we'll move to the positive and show you how to write a clear, succinct resume. First, a number of common errors that crop up all too frequently:

Too wordy. Some of us love to gush and shower the reader with a plethora of hollow adjectives. It's easier writing a wordy resume, highlighting every experience you had on your last job, than highlighting only the important details. The length of your resume and choice of words are critical. Concise resumes are easier to read and remember. Wordy resumes have to be deciphered, which decreases your chances of being considered. We'll get into choice of words shortly. For now, remember that your resume is a condensation, or summation of you. It is not a memoir recounting your work history from year one.

Too short/too long. The trick is to compose a resume that is just the right length—a lean, telling resume that states your story and stops, without bloated adjectives or skeletal thoughts that leave the reader hanging. How long should a resume be? As long as it takes to tell your story. Some resumes are a page, others require two and three pages to cover all the salient points.

Not enough detail. Many resume writers don't know the difference between important and unimportant details. You must learn to make that distinction. Most of us can recall numerous details from our assorted work experiences. Your good memory is not going to get you a job. Your ability to recall significant events might, however. The hard part about writing the job experience section of your resume is isolating critical facts and expounding on them. Cut through the layers of fat and get to the meat. This is what employers are looking for. Not sentence upon sentence, but fact upon fact.

Pretentious. Pretentious resumes make wild claims and are full of unjustified and unsubstantiated thoughts. They focus on the wrong issues, highlighting topics applicants think will impress the reader, rather than sticking to blood-and-guts facts that concentrate on saleable aspects of their background.

Amateurish. Amateurish resumes fall short of the mark. They're half-heartedly prepared, inconsistent, and poorly targeted. What chance do you think they have?

Poor presentation. Just like school, neatness counts. If you don't think it does, send out a smudged, sloppily reproduced resume and see how far it gets you. A personnel representative might read it, but before he's gotten to the experience part, his mind is elsewhere. No matter how brilliant the prose, a sloppy presentation will kill your chances. The paper you use, typewriter, and reproduction process are almost as vital as the information included. We'll get into presentation in more detail later on, but for now realize that a resume is a complete package. Would you walk into a job interview wearing jeans, sneakers, and a polo shirt?

Poor construction (punctuation, grammar, spelling). Recruiters and personnel representatives are flooded with resumes that are chock full of every grammatical, spelling, and punctuation error you can think of. Just as presentation counts, so does mastery of the English language. You don't have to be an honors English student to turn out a grammatically correct resume. All that's required are time, concentration, and a dictionary.

Inaccurate and false statements. It's easy to falsify a resume. All it takes is a little cunning. To make themselves more attractive, job applicants have knocked anywhere from three to ten years off their ages, concocted elaborate job descriptions and titles, and for icing on the cake, added bachelor's and master's degrees from prestigious schools. It's your resume, and you can put anything you want in it. But why take chances and run the risk of being caught?

Surprisingly, most companies do only a cursory check of an applicant's past record, according to a recent survey conducted by the Chicago-based

Hodge, Cronin and Associates, Inc. "We have long suspected that industry was rather indifferent about fraudulent college degree claims," says Hodge, Cronin's president, Richard J. Cronin. "So we decided to determine the extent and impact of this attitude to help us advise our clients."

The survey questionnaires were directed to 440 vice presidents or directors of personnel representing a cross-section of large and medium-size manufacturers, financial institutions, retail chains, and major industries. Fifty-one percent revealed that they only "occasionally or hardly ever" checked college credits. Some of the finest and well-entrenched business institutions in this country only do a half-hearted job of checking on job candidates.

Cronin is appalled by the situation. "The Harvard University registrar's office indicates that out of 50 graduates reference requests each week, three to five of the individuals involved will have no record of having attended the school," he says.

While Cronin's survey revealed a surprisingly naive and indifferent attitude by the majority of American firms in their acceptance of college degree claims without verification, parodoxically, they were quite emphatic about what to do with those who were caught lying. Better than 80 percent of the respondents said they would fire executives who falsely claimed academic degrees. And what if you work within a tightly knit industry where everyone knows one another and an employee's credentials can be checked in moments. When you weigh the pros and cons of trying to get away with falsifying your resume, it's not worth the risk. If caught, the repercussions could seriously mar your chances of getting anywhere in your career.

Vague objective. Think of the objective as the resume's head, and the job experience section its shoulders and torso. The amount of words used in the objective is not the crucial issue. More important is having an objective that stands by itself and needs no explanation. If the reader is unsure about what you want after reading your objective, you'll be lucky if you are called in for an interview.

Resume Writing Style

Everyone approaches the resume differently. The language and style used differs from applicant to applicant. Yet, all well-constructed resumes share common traits. Uppermost is a strong, positive style. Each sentence must be a goal-oriented declarative statement designed to win the reader over. Within seconds the reader must know that you've got the necessary credentials to be successful at your career.

Think of yourself, not as an ordinary job seeker faced with the tedious task of putting together a resume, but as a copywriter, facing the challenging task of writing copy that sells a product. The product is *you*, a subject you're well versed in.

Why a copywriter and not just an ordinary writer? Because a copywriter is a special kind of writer trained to think in short, enticing, telegraph-type sentences. A magazine writer, for example, may have more than 3,000 words to get the message across, a newspaper columnist, 1,000 words. A copywriter, on the other hand, may be limited to under 100 words to make the point and arouse reader or listener interest. Take a close look at some of the print ads that appear in national magazines and newspapers. Whether the ad is trying to sell washing machines, toothpaste, or breakfast cereal, the best of them are written in a sparkling, terse, and inviting style. They're designed to sell. Many of them are not only well written, but witty as well. The next time you turn on your television or radio, listen closely to the ads. Within 10 to 20 seconds, a good ad arouses your interest and curiosity.

The person responsible for writing superior, selling copy is the copywriter, a challenging job indeed. Most of us are not going to be copywriters, but for the time it takes to put together your resume, I urge you to think like one.

Establishing the Right Tone

In the process of playing copywriter, your resume, like a print or TV ad, must accomplish the following goals: communicate, persuade, sell, and have maximum impact. How do you achieve all that? Let's start with resume tone. Depending upon who you are, your background, and the job you're seeking, most applicants adopt one of four tones: academic/formal, conversational, vernacular, or bureaucratic. The academic/formal tone relies on weighty thoughts and sentences to impress the reader. Big words are tossed around like lead weights and sentences are long and unwieldly. Unless you're applying for a job as a college instructor or nuclear physicist, I don't recommend this tone. It's stilted, rigid, and dull.

An example of the academic/formal tone is: "As research director of the company's expanding new product division, my duties included coordinating multimillion dollar research projects, supervising staff of eight electrical engineers, and monitoring expenditures so that they didn't exceed budgetary limitations."

That's a mouthful. It's too long, and it's bloated with words like "coordinating," "monitoring," and "limitations."

Conversational and vernacular tones are a lot lighter and easier to read. They avoid heavy words, focusing on short, digestible sentences. For example, the above illustration using a conversational tone can be reduced to: "Research director/new products. Created and directed large research projects, supervised staff of eight engineers, kept tight reins on budget."

The difference is noticeable. Both job descriptions say the same thing, yet one is cumbersome and hard to swallow and the other is a fast, easy read.

A conversational tone works well in resumes, but be careful with a purely vernacular style. Here you can run into problems. A vernacular style uses slang words or words and phrases that may be popular in one part of the country and unheard of in another. Without realizing it, you run the risk of turning off your reader.

A bureaucratic tone is similar to the academic/formal tone, only it's weighted with lofty titles, initials, and job descriptions indigenous to a particular company or institution. In true bureaucratic style, the reader struggles through a work experience section, barely understanding the terminology.

Occasionally, you'll find resumes that are slickly written, trying to impress the reader with humor and dry wit. If you are a frustrated comedian, save your humor for less important writing ventures. The resume is not the place for cutesy writing.

The ideal tone is one I've dubbed the resume patois, a cross between a conversational and formal tone, with just the right degree of professionalism. A formal/academic tone is too stilted, a vernacular/conversational tone too breezy, but a conversational tone elevated to a professional level with just enough formality is just what the doctor ordered.

Most resumes are far too formal. They read like legal documents, and when really dull, like funeral announcements. Breezy, vernacular-style resumes are not that common, since resumes, by their very nature, have to be ultra serious and professional-sounding. So you can appreciate the importance of experimenting with the resume patois, a style that is both readable and professional. Let's look at this style closely and find out what it is and how to use it.

Style Tips

The resume patois allows a great deal of latitude, and the reader doesn't have to struggle through pointless technical terminology and an unending barrage of oversized adjectives. The idea is to keep the prose flowing, informative, and maintain reader interest. Consider the following pointers:

Don't be a name dropper. Titles or initials tacked on after a name are impressive. But if they're not common titles or initials, don't use them. Many industries have titles and initials few people have heard of. There is nothing wrong with listing your credentials. Don't assume your reader is familiar with your industry and the job you performed. Unless it's a common title, explain it. If your title was director of special services division, don't stop there. Special services means different things to different industries. It sounds impressive, but the first question to be answered is, What is special services division? And as director, what did you do?

Leave nothing to the imagination. Job titles and responsibilities vary from company to company. An administrative supervisor may be in charge of 250 workers at IBM and 12 workers at the International Widget Company. What may appear to be a superfluous job title in a large company could be a senior position in a smaller company. Start from zero position and assume your reader knows nothing about you, your company, and job responsibilities. Your goal is to explain, highlight facts, and stimulate interest.

What are you trying to say? Before scribbling your thoughts on paper, think about what you want to say. Don't expect to knock out a resume in a couple of hours. Learn to think in crisp, descriptive sentences. As we said earlier, each sentence does not have to be a wordy opus worthy of a Faulkner novel. Experiment with different kinds of sentences; long versus short, for example. Or when applicable, use a sentence followed by a series of phrases. By altering your sentence structure, you are making your resume easier to read.

Imagine you're applying for an executive sales position. You worked at your last job for 15 years and during that period accomplished a great deal. Instead of highlighting your accomplishments with a number of sentences, telegraph the facts as follows:

Eastern Sales Manager, Johnson Manufacturing Co., Inc., 45 North Grove Street, Cedar Falls, Michigan, July 1967–Present.

Joined company as a part-time salesman and within two years was promoted to supervising sales manager in charge of the Northwest region. After increasing regional sales by 53 percent, three years after joining company was promoted to sales manager. In 1973 was promoted to executive vice president in charge of sales, and over a nine-year period accomplished the following:

- Increased sales nationwide by 45 percent over a five-year period.
- Instituted cost-saving telemarketing system, reducing sales staff by 15 percent.
- Designed advanced widget, which gained favorable market response within two months.
- Formulated company's first pension plan for lower echelon supervisory staff, creating greater job security, thus significantly reducing employee turnover.

You're not limited to one writing style. Find one that best expresses and summarizes you. The above example is only an illustration, yet is an effective way to list your accomplishments. In seconds the reader can run through the above worker's accomplishments and understand precisely what this person did in 15 years with the company. After introducing himself, he summarizes the key points of his last position in list-type fashion. It's a perfect place to use a phrase instead of a sentence. It's also easier to read and saves space.

Think logically. Don't list accomplishments and job descriptions at random. List them in a meaningful order. Show a progression of events. Recruiters are curious to know how and at what pace you maneuvered through the ranks. If you started off as a runner and within eight years were promoted five times, list each major promotion, title, and job description.

Highlight Accomplishments

Toot your horn in a tasteful manner. The personnel person reading your resume wants to know about your accomplishments. Saying you instituted "cost-saving sales techniques, reduced overhead costs, and was single-handedly responsible for creating the company's most advanced and hard-hitting advertising program" tells the reader nothing concrete. It sounds great, but what does it mean? What cost-saving sales techniques were instituted? How were overhead costs reduced? How did that advanced hard-hitting ad program affect the company?

"An employer not only wants to know what you did, but how well you did it," insists Mike Keough of ExecuSearch. "Often, job applicants don't put their accomplishments down. And if they do list them, they're often covered up in smoke."

An advertising copywriter described part of her job functions this way: "My copy appealed to clients and investors because I concentrated on new products and improvements. I created a new editorial philosophy that allowed for greater productivity and creativity on the part of the copywriters. Under a new system I developed, the agency was able to present new clients with the outline of a campaign within 24 hours after a first meeting."

The above job description is another example of ineffectual writing. On first reading it sounds great. But after a second read, you realize you were snowed. First she says her copy appealed to clients and investors because she concentrated on new products and improvements. The statement sounds impressive, but how do we know this person's copy appealed to clients and investors? No evidence is presented to back this up. Next, she says she fashioned an editorial philosophy that allowed for greater productivity and creativity. Another hollow statement. What was the editorial philosophy? How did it work? How did it promote greater productivity and creativity? Lastly, she mentions a new system which allowed her agency to present clients with an outline of an ad campaign within 24 hours after a first meeting. Wonderful. But what was the new system all about and how did it work? Missing are hard facts. The writing is subjective, opinionated, and self-oriented. An experienced personnel executive will see right through it. Your task is to build a solid case for yourself, and it can be accomplished easily by layering fact upon fact. Pretend you're the employer or personnel manager for a moment. As personnel manager, the umbrella question to be answered before hiring someone is, Why is this person right for the job?

Listing hollow job functions is not the way. Anyone can do that. Instead, think in terms of a cause-and-effect relationship. If you instituted a new program, designed something, revamped a department, what effect did it all have on company sales, revenues, products, employees, etc.?

There is nothing wrong with some tasteful boasting about your background and accomplishments. Just make sure every statement can be backed by facts.

Picking the Right Words

Any words won't do. Find the right ones that advertise your talents. As we said earlier in this chapter, wordy resumes are deadly. And so are resumes gorged with big words. Use short action words that describe your job functions in the simplest, most effective way. Note the wording from the following sample resume.

In my three years with the company, a few noteworthy accomplishments were:

- Increased productivity of my department 50 percent by reducing needless overhead expenses.
- Redesigned distribution network, increasing widget sales by 35 percent.
- Instituted incentive bonus system, thus reducing employee turnover 20 percent.

The above writer chose her words carefully. Anyone reading this job description knows at a glance *what she did* and *how well she did it*.

While action words are preferable to passive words and phrases, don't overuse them. When possible substitute them with facts. Words like *implemented, organized, planned, improved, produced, supervised, conducted, operated*, need no explanation. Use them properly. Merely saying you produced, supervised, conducted, or operated something is only part of the story. Most important is how well you performed these tasks.

Finally, write your resume in the first person. For some inexplicable reason many resume writers shy away from the first person. Maybe they feel it's too boastful. But this is no time for false modesty. The resume is all about you, and the better it captures you in a strong, positive light, the better your chances of landing a good job.

Some people write their resume in the third person. Instead of "I," it's "Mr. Jones," or just "Jones," or simply, "he." Third person resumes sound stilted and are to be avoided.

The personal pronoun "I" is preferred, but try not to overuse it. Too much repetition can be tedious. A recommended approach is to introduce a section in the first person and then list your accomplishments in short bulletlike phrases. For example:

As manager of the research division, I instituted the following changes:

- Redesigned house organ from a 24-page magazine to a 10-page newsletter, resulting in an annual savings of $50,000.
- Instituted fact-checking system, reducing published errors by 90 percent.
- Saved company $200,000 a year by printing annual reports in-house, as opposed to using commercial printing house.

Where there is a will, there is a way. Experiment with different forms, tones, and writing styles. Don't be content with the first thing you scribble on paper. Not only do you have to pretend you're a copywriter, but an editor as well. Once you've picked the words that highlight your important accomplishments, pare your prose so that only the lean facts are left. As editor of your resume, you have to decide which words work, which to delete, and how to keep the language tight and readable.

I know you're in a mad rush to get that special job. But be practical and farsighted. You don't have to be a great writer to produce a winning resume. All you have to do is put some time, effort, and work into the project, and you'll be delighted with the results.

eight

Choosing a Resume Format

It's time to shift into second gear and pick an appropriate resume format, one that best serves you. The four basic resume formats are: chronological, functional, combination (all-purpose), and entry-level. They still serve most job seekers' needs. However, this complex, changing job market has created new problems for job seekers. The unemployment rate is high, industries are retooling plants and closing down others, outmoded job functions are being phased out to be replaced by newer ones, workers are changing career directions midstream, while other workers are reentering the job force after a long absence. Hence, we have an intricate and volatile job climate, creating a need for better and expanded resumes.

Along with the four basic resume styles, we'll also discuss the resume alternative letter, which is ideal for applicants who don't fit the traditional resume mold.

Let's take it from the top and start with the chronological resume.

Chronological Resume

It's not hard to see why this is the most popular resume format. It is easy to set up and read, and if you have two or more years of work experience under your belt, the chronological resume may be your best bet. As its name implies, it lists work and educational experience in order of time. It begins with your most recent position and works backwards. There is no mystery to this form. In seconds an employer can scan your two to fifteen years of work history and have a global picture of what you're all about.

For the majority of applicants, the chronological resume is suggested. At its best, it is a well-documented fact sheet of who you are and where you are going. It has traditionally served as the most logical resume format for the following reasons:

- It presents a career continuum in a logical, understandable order.
- It focuses on specific jobs and functions.
- It's ideal for the candidate who knows exactly what he/she wants.

Despite its popularity, the chronological format may not be the best vehicle for you. Its shortcomings lie in the tendency to emphasize the following:

- Disorientation and inability to hold a job for long periods of time, if you've had many jobs.
- Changed career objectives.
- Sameness of routines from one job to another.
- If you've been out of the work force for a long period of time.

Keep the above factors in mind before settling on the chronological format. Whatever resume style you choose, make sure it works for you, not against you. Remember, the perfect resume is the one that gets you the job you're shooting for.

Let's take a look at a couple of chronological resumes.

PERSONNEL MANAGER

Jesse Steward
2131 South Street
North Park, Ohio 44701
(216) 890-7765

Summary of
Experience

Wide-ranging background in corporate relations and recruitment of middle-level and top-level management. Experience gained through employment with large chemical and industrial companies.

Objective

To work for large, growing company where my background in industrial relations can be used to good advantage.

Employment
History

Laker Industrial Corporation
239 Johnson Drive
East Mansfield, Ohio

1975–Present

Personnel manager for industrial corporation with subsidiaries and branch offices throughout the midwestern states. Company recorded consistent sales of over $800 million annually. Started as associate personnel manager and within two years was promoted to full manager with a staff of 15 under me. Broad-based job functions included creating employment strategies for employees, from unskilled entry-level workers to senior management. Responsible for negotiating union contracts, creating employee benefits program, and negotiating bonus system for midde-level management.

1970–1975   Atlas Manufacturing, Inc.
                 76 Juniper Road
                 Manofield, Ohio

                 Employment manager for the largest manufacturer of computer relays. Company posts average annual sales exceeding $100 million a year. Responsibilities included recruitment of middle- and top-echelon executives as well as supervision of lower-level supervisory workers. Negotiated union contracts and created two major incentive work programs.

1964–1970   Brighton Typewriter Corporation
                 45 Lake Forest Drive
                 Mansfield, Ohio

                 Field recruitment officer for regional typewriter manufacturing company with offices in eight states. Working directly with home office executives, responsibilities included hiring supervisory personnel along with skilled and entry-level employees. Administered personnel policies from home office and supervised employees' medical, insurance, and incentive programs.

Education   Rutgers University, bachelor's degree, personnel psychology, 1959; postgraduate work at Fordham University in labor relations, industrial management

Foreign   Fluent in French
Language

Personal   Married/four children

COPYWRITER

Joan Thornton
45 High Street
South Point, New Jersey 07114
(201) 678-6548

Objective   Copywriting position that capitalizes on my extensive knowledge of women's fashion industry.

Employment   Longley, Druid and Bush Advertising
History   348 Madision Avenue
                 New York, N.Y.

1978–Present   Copy chief on three major fashion accounts. With staff of four copywriters, supervised all copy before it was sent to clients for approval. The accounts' total yearly advertising budget exceeded $8 million a year. Aside from administrative functions, I designed and prepared ad campaign for largest account.

1972–1978	Belton Advertising 221 Fifth Avenue New York, N.Y. Copywriter for Druid Dress, the largest women's dress company in United States. Reported to copy chief, but had sole control over this $12 million account. Wrote all copy for national print campaign and supervised regional TV and radio ad campaign as well.
1968–1972	Elton, Grave, Dirge, Inc. 87 Park Avenue New York, N.Y. Began at bottom in backup/gofer position, and within 10 months was an assistant copywriter with some say in editorial production. After outlining and creating extensive regional ad campaign for Beatrice Dress Company, was promoted to copywriter, reporting directly to agency's copy chief. In less than two years' time, was functioning on my own. Conceived the ad program for this high-exposure dress company and wrote all the copy. In my last year with company, along with copywriting responsibilities, assisted the account executive on the account. Had a say in all aspects of running the account, from conception and design to launching campaign.
Education	Smith College, bachelor's degree, English, 1966; Columbia University, postgraduate courses in writing advertising copy, production, and account management, 1968.
Affiliations	Long-standing member of Advertising Council of America. As member of standards committee, I have a voice in creating fair and ethical business practices among advertising agencies throughout the United States.
Personal	Married/one child

Note that the chronological-type samples are pretty much the same in terms of basic form. The noticeable difference is that one has a summary of experience, the other doesn't. There is no firm rule here. Some resume writers think it improves their chances if they summarize their work experience at the very top. It's an optional heading. Depending upon your objectives, it can either work for you or against you. If your goals are obvious, it's not necessary. If they're vague, it can confuse the reader.

Most chronological resumes list an objective below applicant's name and address. This is more common than a summary of experience. Some resumes with clearly implied objectives bypass the objective as well. Again, it depends upon what kind of a job you are after and how well your resume is written. As a general rule, it's a good idea to take no chances and list an objective.

The problem with the summary of experience is that applicants overload the section with cliches, and run off at the mouth with adjectivitis. If you use it, keep it brief.

Finally, if you are modifying your career direction, special attention should be paid to your job objective. As soon as possible, tell the reader you are "broadening your career spectrum," "changing direction," "encompassing new ground." Don't leave the reader hanging. Your resume is not supposed to read like a mystery novel. If you're saving the punch line for last, you, not the reader, are in for a surprise.

Functional Resume

The functional resume stresses function, rather than chronology. While it is not as popular as the chronological resume, the form has some distinct advantages often overlooked by job seekers.

In this job market especially, the functional resume can be a more enticing vehicle for displaying your talents and abilities. If you're what the personnel recruiters call a job hopper, someone who changes jobs frequently, you'd do well to consider the functional format. The chronological format is not recommended because it highlights each job. Without a word in your defense, you're branded as unstable. Whereas, if strategically disguised within a functional format, the reader concentrates on your accomplishments, rather than coming to any rash conclusions before reading the entire resume. Inevitably, he gets to the chronology of jobs at the bottom of the resume and by that time, hopefully, he is favorably impressed.

If the functional resume is well constructed, it can predispose a personnel worker in the applicant's favor. The byword is *strategy*. Often, it's not so much the information you present, but *how* you present it, which accounts for the strength of one resume over another.

The advantages of the functional resume are as follows:

1. Essentially contains same information as chronological resume, but presents it under an expanded format. Applicants have the opportunity to go into more detail, concentrating on job function and how they maneuvered themselves through the ranks.
2. Gives applicants chance to tell how well they did their jobs.
3. Enables applicants to minimize certain aspects of their past, such as a spotty employment record.
4. Is an excellent format if changing careers or altering career direction. Through narrative sections of functional format, applicants can point up skills, traits, and abilities that are ideal for a career move.

Let's say you worked as a systems analyst for 15 years and feel it's time to shift gears and move into computer sales. It's a logical change in career direction. The question is what is the most effective way to initiate that change? How do you highlight your knowledge of computers, the computer industry, your ability to work effectively with people, and your desire to move into sales? Certainly not with a chronological resume. A chronological format will paint you as a disoriented applicant who, after working as a systems analyst for a number of years, suddenly decides to change career direction and try sales. In contrast, the functional format gives you the opportunity to show that the transition from systems analysis to computer sales is logical, practical, and finally, that you're the ideal candidate for the transition.

5. Recommended for applicants with large gaps in their employment record. While dates of employment are included in the resume, they assume a subordinate status over capabilities and job skills.

Word of caution. Don't misuse the functional format. Personnel managers are word detectives when it comes to separating fact from fiction. Don't use it to avoid giving concrete information or to snow employers with trivial information.

Following are two sample functional resumes. The second is in skeletal form.

PUBLIC RELATIONS

Peter Hambone
65 Hammermill Lane
South Ambuke, Tennessee 38166
(901) 998-2972

Writing
Well versed in all aspects of public relations writing. Over the past 10 years, handled wide-ranging public relations assignments, incuding report, speech, and release writing. Also, prepared articles for company newsletters, house organs, and annual reports. The assignments ranged from gathering information, checking facts, to preparing the finished product.

Editing/Proofreading
All material written by staff members or myself was carefully edited. Involved a multistage process whereby copy was edited and proofed by staff members before I went over it. In final stage, I reread and approved all copy before it was sent to client.

Production
In the final stage of preparing copy, supervised entire production process, regardless of the type of publication being produced. Possess a thorough knowledge of production methods as well as a working knowledge of typefaces and paper grades. Also capable of single-handedly laying out magazine and sizing and cropping photos to dimensions of page.

Account Liaison
Thorough working knowledge of account executive functions. Whether working for a nonprofit, fund-raising, or corporate account, worked with clients from the inception of an idea, development of program, to putting the wheels in motion. Enjoy working on a one-to-one basis with clients.

Employment History
1980–Present	Public relations, writer, Litcomb & Benedict, West Ambuke, Tennessee
1979–1980	Account executive/writer, Joyce Elwood, Ltd., South Ambuke, Tennessee

1976–1979	Account executive, Litchfield and Brayson, Inc., South Ambuke, Tennessee
1972–1976	Staff assistant/researcher, Selzer & Selzer, Memphis, Tennessee
1970–1972	Public relations trainee, A.W. Horthorne, Inc., Memphis, Tennessee

Education
Bachelor's degree, Hofstra University, 1968
Master's degree, Columbia University, 1970

Foreign Language   Speak Spanish fluently

Personal
Married/one child

Jessica L. Brockhead

9087 Clifford Drive   (413) 987-8876
West Hampshire, Massachusetts 01238

CHEMICAL ENGINEER

Achievements
—Coordinated $4 million cost-saving ....
—Initiated incentive program cutting costs ....
—Organized extensive chemical waste-removal system for pollution-free
—Tested and refined new fuel extract ....
—Supervised cost-saving program that resulted in a savings ....
—Increased company's chemical output, producing a net sales increase ..

Employment

Jacobs Chemical Extract	1978–Present
Senior Engineer/Administrator	

Lipcomb Chemicals, Inc.	1974–1978
Senior Chemical Engineer	

Bryce, Hemlock Chemical, Ltd.	1970–1974
Chemical Engineer	

Education

University of Wisconsin, Bachelor of Science, 1968

Professional Affiliations

American Society of Chemical Engineers, charter member, vice president since 1978

Personal

Single

When structuring your functional format, make it as readable as possible. In the skeletal sample, note the use of action introductory words in the achievements section. This makes for impressive reading. The reader's eyes are riveted on power words like *coordinated, initiated, organized, tested, supervised,* and *increased.* The phrases are short, and the reader remembers the applicant as a doer, starter, initiator, and hard worker.

All-purpose, or Combination, Resume

The all-purpose, or combination, resume is a hybrid form merging the chronological and functional approaches into one format. It can be an excellent selling tool for an applicant who's been in the work force a number of years and whose marketability can be affirmed on a number of fronts. Like the chronological format, it is suitable for applicants who have strong work backgrounds and who are striving for better positions within their fields.

Following are some sample combination resumes.

SALES DIRECTOR

Larry Benchley
89 Litcomb Avenue
San Francisco, California 94818
(415) 765-8827

Objective

Position as sales director of expanding multidivision company.

Achievements

Management

Directed and coordinated $5 million sales program. Single-handedly made policy decisions concerning all aspects of sales activities.

Market
Strategy

—Analyzed and investigated market in order to stay abreast of current trends.
—Developed sales strategies that could be statistically controlled and tested on regional basis.
—Created program based upon controlled, staggered selling with strong regional orientation.

Merchandising

Kept close tabs on merchandising departments to develop cost-effective programs that promoted products via point-of-purchase displays.

Sales Incentives

Created sales incentive programs to promote sales on a company-wide basis. Salespeople are encouraged to increase sales effort for lucrative rewards, including bonuses, paid vacations; sustained sales records were rewarded with promotions.

Sales Training

Created unified company-wide sales strategies. Salespeople along with sales executives attend monthly sales meetings where sales procedures are studied and analyzed in order to create more profitable techniques.

Work History

1972–Present   Hawthorne Cosmetics, Inc.
                   908 Hawthorne Lane
                   San Francisco, California

Sales Director   With staff of 15, directed entire sales effort of this $300 million company, with branches and subsidiaries throughout the world. Over an eight-year period, consolidated regional sales efforts, created unified selling procedures, and increased company sales by 35 percent.

1963–1972   Congrove Brush, Inc.
                   76 Robin Road
                   San Francisco, California

Sales Coordinator Began as sales trainee and over 10-year period worked my way through company ranks to position of sales coordinator, second in command to sales director. Helped formulate new selling strategies and cost-effective sales programs.

Education   Bachelor's degree, University of Southern California, 1962

Personal   Married/two children

URBAN DESIGNER

Louise Bryant
76 Haldale Lane
West Hartford, Connecticut 06061
(203) 876-5541

Expertise
Twenty years experience as urban planner/architect. Qualified to handle wide-ranging problems in urban development. Created number of successful programs for overhauling, rehabilitating, and redesigning decaying sections of surrounding neighborhoods. Working with government agencies and carefully selected contractors, decaying neighborhoods were torn down and reconstructed to give way to renovated areas that fused residential and commercial properties, thus making the areas profitable and habitable at the same time.

Education
Princeton University, B.S. Architecture, 1965
Columbia University, M.S. Urban Design, 1967

Affiliations
President of American Urban Planning Association, the national association for urban redevelopment. Over a five-year period, created several fund-raising drives and doubled membership.

Experience
Johnson & Associates, Ltd. Hartford, Conn. 1975–Present

Project Director
Responsible for designing the $15 million Hawthorne Housing Project in
Bay section of Hartford. This was a major undertaking requiring the
rehousing and redistribution of 3,000 people to safe, controlled housing.
Had a major part of every facet of mammoth project. Work was satisfac-
torily completed, on schedule, to city's specifications, $45,000 under budget.

Sanders & Sanders, Inc., New York City, 1971–1975

Project Coordinator
Designed and supervised construction of a three-building office complex in
lower Manhattan, which was part of a major urban redevelopment program.
Meeting rigid city requirements, made sure effort proceeded on schedule
and satisfied state and city zoning requirements. Worked with large staff
and reported directly to project director.

Harris, Farnom & Wadsworth, New York City, 1967–1971

Urban Designer
Gained valuable experience designing factories, office buildings, and a two-
acre state-funded park in an inner-city neighborhood. Broad experience in
design, planning, coordination, budgeting, and working with corporate and
government agencies. Made sure contractors kept to schedules and monitored expenditures so projects didn't exceed tight budgets.

Personal
Married/two children

Entry-Level Resume

Let's hope that one enlightened day high school and college administrators
will insist graduating classes take an all-inclusive course in job-hunting
techniques. As we rub elbows with the 21st century, it's imperative that
job applicants have all the necessary tools to get the jobs they've trained
so hard for. As Mike Keough of ExecuSearch says, "We teach people skills,
yet we don't teach them the techniques necessary to get the jobs that will
utilize those skills."

Writing an ordinary resume is difficult enough, but preparing an entry-
level resume can be an aggravating experience from start to finish. With
no real or long-term work experience to boast about, it can be a challenging chore. You are anxious to get a job, and you're forced to stare at a
blank piece of white paper, trying to conjure up relevant facts and figures
that will entice an employer.

Most entry-level resumes are awful. They're dashed off, chock full of
typos and inconsistencies, and bloated with trivial information.

Common errors found in many entry-level resumes are:

1. Lack of realistic objective
2. Unfocused, irrelevant information
3. Failure to highlight strengths

1. Lack of realistic objective. Not all graduating seniors (high school or college) know what they want to do with their lives. They lack a clearly focused goal (or goals). It helps if you know exactly where you're headed, but it's not the end of the world if you don't. If you don't know what you want to be doing a decade down the road, don't put down the first thing that pops into your head. Putting something nebulous down for a career objective, such as "Looking for a growth-oriented position leading to a senior-level management position," will get you a big yawn and a hasty dismissal to the unusable file.

Put some effort into your resume and come up with an objective that makes sense and that is consistent with your school experience. If you have a degree in accounting, don't put systems analyst for your job objective. Or if you graduated with a degree in finance, don't write president of a bank for your objective.

What should you say? Whatever you write, be consistent and brief. Job recruiters don't expect long-winded, flowery objectives from a recent college or high school graduate. All they expect is a job objective that is an outgrowth of your training.

Let's say you have a bachelor's degree in English and your goal is to build a career in publicity or public relations. A sensible career objective might be, "Association with a firm where my educational background can be utilized in the field of publicity and promotion." Or with a business administration degree, a logical career objective is: "To gain experience working for a large firm, eventually working into a position with general management responsibilities." Both objectives make sense. They're simple, clearly stated, telling a potential employer exactly what you hope to get from a job. Holding a business administration degree and saying you want to be president of a bank can be likened to saying you want to be president of the United States after serving as class president.

Don't put the cart before the horse. There is nothing wrong with wanting to be president of a bank. But be logical and clear headed. As we said in Chapter Four, personnel directors are looking for applicants with consistent and logical goals. If your goal is to be a bank president, outline the steps necessary to attain that position and list the appropriate entry-level job that will put you on the right track.

2. Unfocused, irrelevant information. Don't fill your resume with trivial information. Keep it pertinent and career oriented. If you're looking for a job in public relations, advertising, or as an automotive technician, don't mention that you were a member of the chess club, took belly dancing, or taught a course in transcendental meditation. No doubt you learned a lot, but a prospective employer couldn't care less. However, if you were a reporter or editor of your school newspaper, or a member of the advertising club, or took an advanced class in automotive repair, that's relevant information placing you in sharp relief. Better yet, if you are involved in an internship program or work-study program in your career area, by all means highlight this information on your resume. It's pertinent, relevant, and increases your chances of getting the job.

3. Failure to highlight strengths. Personnel directors don't expect long, detailed resumes for entry-level jobs. They're well aware that recent college or high school graduates have little, if any, work experience. Their selling points are their academic credentials or vocational skills. If you fall into this category, keep your resume tight, pointed, and concentrated on your strengths and skills developed thus far. Use the following sample resumes as your guide.

> Ellen F. Brando
> 987 Dunhill Drive
> Concord, New Hampshire 03301
> (603) 987-9987

Objective
Accounting staff position with a large corporation which allows me to develop skills learned in college. Plan on continuing my education in order to become a certified public accountant.

Work Experience (Part-time/Summer)

Louis C. Bender, C.P.A.   September 1981–June 1982
North Concord, New Hampshire

Working part-time during school year, attained practical experience assisting an established C.P.A. Helped prepare financial statements, record transactions, perform bookkeeping functions, and gather data. At tax time, worked with firm's clients preparing IRS returns. Working with different types of accounts, got practical experience in the prudent handling of clients' accounts.

Jason, Heller & Brodlie, Inc.   May 1980–September 1980
Concord, New Hampshire

Performed mostly bookkeeping functions for general accounting firm. Some client contact, and a great deal of fact checking, including gathering data for balance sheet statements.

Department of Tax Collection,
City of Concord   May 1979–September 1979
Concord, New Hampshire

Part of large city comptroller's staff. Worked in bill and tax collection department updating and keeping track of delinquent accounts. Processed late income tax returns.

Educational Background
University of New Hampshire, Bachelor of Business Administration, 1982. Major, accounting; Minor, statistics.

Personal
Single

Terrence T. Grady
78 Willis Avenue
Teaneck, New Jersey 07666
(201) 877-7728

Objective
Association with company with programming/computer department where
I can use my technical background and mathematical and organizational
skills. By mastering all aspects of programming, installation, and systems
design, my goal is to work into systems analysis.

Work Experience (Summer)

Brandt International, Inc.   (Summer, 1980)
Fort Lee, New Jersey

Programming Assistant
Excellent ground-floor opportunity where I gained a working knowledge
of basic computer systems and their installation. By working with experienced technicians, I got hands-on experience installing computers.

International Software, Inc.   (Summer, 1979)
Passaic, New Jersey

Field Assistant
Working with experienced installers, the greater part of the day consisted
of assisting with the installation of computer systems. The systems ranged
from small systems with uncomplicated terminal hookups to major systems
requiring a team of three and four technicians. Learned nuts and bolts of
installation work, and the special problems and challenges of wiring a
system. Worked against a rigid schedule, where installations had to be set
up or repaired at customer's convenience.

Digital Hardware, Inc.   (Summer, 1978)
New York City

Parts Handler And Coder
Part of large assembly line, responsibilities included inspecting computer
chips, coding them, packaging and preparing orders. Learned how computer
parts are mass-produced and shipped all over the world. Since speed and
accuracy were vital, I developed workable systems so orders could be
processed accurately and on schedule.

Educational Background
Polytechnical Institute of New York, Bachelor of Science, 1981.
Majored in computer science, minored in math.

Professional Affiliation
Active member of International Data Processing Society

Personal
Single

Lawrence O'Hara
8 Oliver Road
Windsor, Vermont 05089
(802) 876-8862

Objective
Junior mechanic in growing automotive shop where I can work into a supervisory position.

Work Experience (Part-time/Summer)

J & L Auto   May 1981–September 1982
Bristol, Vermont

Under close supervision of shop foreman, was shop's mechanic/helper. Assisting experienced mechanics in different phases of automotive repair, helped with minor repairs, replaced broken parts, changed tires and worn shocks, and assisted in wheel alignments. Ordered and picked up stock and made sure replacement accounts were in order.

Brice Automotive   May 1980–September 1980
Windsor, Vermont

Assisted three-person staff with minor repairs, from tuning up engines and replacing worn spark plugs and mufflers to test-driving autos after they were repaired. Also assisted in keeping shop's books. Worked irregular hours and often put in seven days a week when regular staff was sick or on vacation.

J & J Sunoco   May 1979–September 1979
Windsor, Vermont

Gas station and automotive repair shop general helper, required to do a little of everything from pumping gas, taking money, filling out charge cards, cleaning cars, to changing windshield wipers, tires, and occasionally replacing a damaged hose under supervision of shop supervisor. At end of day was responsible for watering down work areas and cleaning up shop.

Education
Vermont Academy of Automotive Design, vocational diploma with honors, B-plus average, 1982

Personal
Single

Resume Alternative Letter

The above-mentioned formats work for most job seekers—but not for everyone.

What if you were out of the work force for a number of years? Your children are in school, it's been 10 years since your last outside job, and you're ready to go back. Where do you begin? Or, after working 15 years in a field, you feel it's time to alter your career course and move into a more challenging career. How do you convince an employer you're not an unstable job hopper, but someone who has the background and credentials for the switch? A resume may not be the answer, but a well-written letter telling an employer about your abilities and how you'd be perfect for the job may be the approach to consider.

Why a letter and not a resume? Resumes are summations of past experience, whereas the resume alternative letter minimizes past work experience and concentrates on the future, specifically how you can be of service to an employer.

Warning. Don't think you're getting off easy by using a letter instead of a resume. The letter is only an alternative, or substitute, for the resume and requires the same input necessary for a resume.

Before we outline a model form to follow, consider the following pointers before constructing your letter:

1. Identify need.
2. Research company.
3. Send to individual.
4. Describe your skills, citing specifics; mention references if you can.
5. Keep it brief.
6. Request appointment.

Think of a resume alternative letter as a *here's what I can do for you letter.* The letter must be strong, persuasive, and must capture the reader's attention immediately. Don't forget that it's taking the place of the resume and has to be an equally forceful selling tool. Let's run through the above pointers in more detail.

1. Identify need. Don't send letters out at random. First, identify a need and find employers who are looking for people with your particular talents.

2. Research company. Before you do a first draft of your letter, find out everything you can about the company. Once you know the company's needs, tailor a strong, selling promotional letter. When possible, it doesn't hurt to cite facts and figures, demonstrating that you're more than casually interested, that you've done some research on the company before applying for the job.

3. Send to individual. If you are going to the trouble to write a letter, go one step further and identify the person to send it to, someone who will either hire you or who can put you in touch with the person who can.

4. Describe your skills, citing specifics; mention references. Within the space of a short, selling letter, you have to do a professional selling job on yourself. Don't pussyfoot. Get to the facts as soon as possible. Tell how you can be of service and back it up with significant details from your past. If it's a selling or financial job, mention numbers—how you cut corners, saved an employer money, increased sales.

5. Keep it brief. It may take a few drafts, but keep it tight and brief, preferably a page, two at most. It may take a couple of drafts to shave unnecessary words, but by all means keep it to a discreet length. Assume from the onset that the people you're sending it to are extremely busy and have little time to read letters. A three-page letter may scare a potential employer off, or your letter may be passed on to a subordinate instead of the person in charge.

6. Request appointment. In closing your letter, politely request an appointment, a convenient time you can come in and meet the employer. By mentioning it in the letter, you're leaving nothing to chance. You're saying you are dead serious about working for the company. Or in closing, say that if you don't hear from the company within two weeks, you'll call to request an appointment. It's a shrewd tactic because it forces the employer to act and not relegate your letter to a filing cabinet or a corner of a secretary's desk. By telling the employer you intend to follow up on the letter, he has no choice but to act on the letter and let you know whether he's interested or not.

Let's draft a sample letter. The enclosed letter was written by an ex-teacher who stopped working for 10 years to have children. Her children are in school, and she's ready to go back to work.

On her last job she taught young children and coordinated programs for disadvantaged children from poor neighborhoods. Along with coordinating the programs she also taught and worked closely with the children. Hearing about the opening of a day care center in her area through a friend, she sent the following letter to the director of the program.

June 3, 1982

87 Barclay Street
San Francisco, California 94115
(415) 988-4533

Mr. Charles Bancroft
Bay Street Day Care Center
4508 Bay Street
San Francisco, California 94115

Dear Mr. Bancroft:

Through Jane Bander, an old and dear friend, I learned of your new day care center and your need for qualified, experienced workers to run the program.

I am making my services available to you, because this is a field I am not only qualified to work in, but one which I sincerely love.

I have a great deal of experience working with small children, as a kindergarten and first grade teacher for four years, as a supervisor and coordinator in the federally funded Head Start Program in my district, and finally, as a mother of two growing children. In total, I have over 10 years' experience working with small children, especially disadvantaged children. They have special problems requiring skilled practitioners who can work with them and help them realize their full potential.

As a supervisor and coordinator in the Head Start Program, I designed work/play programs for three-, four-, and five-year-olds and picked, trained, and supervised my staff as well. I enjoyed my work with Head Start. It was gratifying, rewarding, and challenging, all at the same time.

I stopped working when I became pregnant with my first child. Now that my children are school age and don't require my constant attention, I am anxious to return to the work I enjoyed so much. As I said, I feel I am amply qualified to be of assistance to your day care center.

I hold a bachelor's degree from Smith College and a master's degree in social work from Columbia University. I would like to meet with you to discuss in greater detail how I can be of service to you.

My schedule is flexible, and I can meet with you any time at your convenience. If I don't hear from you within 10 days, I will follow this letter up with a phone call.

I look forward to hearing from you.

Sincerely,

Judith Cartwright

Let's take a closer look at Judith Cartwright's letter. If you were Mr. Bancroft, would you respond favorably to the letter? I hope so, because I would if I were in his place.

Secondly, do you think a resume would have been as effective as this letter? Answer: no. A resume would not have been as effective for a number of reasons. Uppermost, the 10-year time gap is played down in the letter. When you finish reading her letter, the fact she was out of the job market for 10 years in no way mars her chances of being considered for the job.

The letter starts off with a personal touch; a friend in common is the reference point for sending the letter. Once introductions are made, she gets to the point. She acknowledges the need for skilled workers, and then goes about focusing her qualifications to the employer's needs. In a professional manner, she lists her past credentials, plus educational background, telling the reader that she is not only amply qualified, but that she thoroughly enjoys her work as well. She makes it clear that if she gets the job, it will be a lot more than a place to hang her hat from nine to five. She even makes her 10-year absence work for her by implying that she owed it to her children to stay home during the crucial childhood years, and that it was a valuable part of her repertory of experiences with young children.

Finally, she tells the reader she intends to follow up on the letter if she doesn't hear anything in 10 days. Her message is loud and clear: she wants the job, is qualified, and wants an interview so she can get to second base and be considered seriously.

The resume alternative letter hits the nail on the head and accomplishes its goal. As an optional tactic, she can enclose an updated resume along with her letter. However, the letter suffices because it's clearly focused and amply serves as a persuasive tool.

Let's look at one more example. Imagine a 20-year auto assembly foreman we'll call Bill Jones losing his job because his Detroit factory pared its staff by 40 percent. One day Bill enjoyed job security and the prospect of a comfortable retirement, and the next day he's on the street looking for a new job. It's bad enough losing your job, but when the job prospects throughout your industry evaporate before your eyes, the world suddenly looks less than appetizing.

What are Bill Jones's options? Does he (1) give up hope of securing a job in his field, (2) try to find a job in an auto plant in another city, or (3) alter his career path by marketing his skills towards an allied industry that can profit from his talents. If you picked number 3, you're thinking like a seasoned career strategist.

He could try to find a job in another auto plant, but with plant closings and layoffs, he's playing Russian roulette with his career. Even if he were lucky enough to secure a job in another plant, it may mean relocating to another city. A far simpler path is to analyze his skills, talents, and experience and look for a job in an allied field.

With 20 years' experience behind him, Bill Jones is more marketable than he realizes. His assets include a working knowledge of gasoline- and diesel-fueled automobiles, assembly line functions, auto body construction, design, maintenance, plus supervisory skills. When he assesses his career options, he can take one of two possible alternative career paths. He can work as a head mechanic/supervisor in an auto repair shop, or possibly as a mechanic jack-of-all-trades/troubleshooter in a boat engine plant or repair shop.

Boats and automobiles are very different. However, the engines that drive them have a lot in common. They operate under the same principles and are similar in construction and design. And since Bill is familiar with both gasoline and diesel engines, he is a potential asset to both a boat engine manufacturer and automaker.

If Bill Jones decides to apply for a job in a boat engine factory, he'd do well to follow Judith Cartwright's lead when she applied for the job in the day care center after being out of work 10 years. He could send a resume instead, but it wouldn't be as effective as the resume alternative letter. A resume would concentrate on his 20 years in an automotive plant, and a prospective employer might not realize that he is capable of transferring and adapting his skills. The letter, on the other hand, acts as a functional bridge relating one job skill to a similar skill in an allied industry.

After researching the job market, he uncovers three boat engine manufacturers who are looking for mechanics. Knowing their needs, he drafts the following resume alternative letter:

June 19, 1982

29 Astor Place
Detroit, Michigan 48203
(313) 201-8968

Mr. Harold M. Fuller
Hawthorne Boat Engines, Inc.
22 Hillsdale Street
Detroit, Michigan 48203

Dear Mr. Fuller:

I understand your company is looking for experienced boat engine mechanics who have a working knowledge of engine repair, construction, and replacement parts.

While I never worked in a boat engine factory, I have 20 years' experience working in Allied Motors's South End plant, where I amassed a working knowledge of auto body construction repair and assembly line functions. I began as an assembler and worked my way into a supervisory capacity, overseeing 150 workers on an assembly line. Aside from monitoring my workers, I was responsible for meeting the plant's tight production schedules.

Over the years, I've worked on both gasoline- and diesel-fueled automobiles. As you know, boat and automobile engines have much in common. Along with a familiarity with auto body construction and maintenance, I can take apart either a gasoline or diesel engine and put it back together in excellent working order. Working in any number of capacities, I can be an asset to your operation.

It's common knowledge these days that auto plants are paring staffs and some have no other recourse but to close marginal plants. Sales are off and the major automakers have to retrench in order to cut overhead costs. Like thousands of other workers, I was laid off when my plant decided to pare its staff by 40 percent. However, I'm delighted to say my work and production record with Allied Motors were excellent, and I'll be more than happy to provide the necessary references to support this.

In view of what's taking place throughout the auto industry, I feel a career move makes a great deal of sense. Your company is a major manufacturer of boat engines worldwide, and I would like to be part of your team and help boost profits. My skills, experience, knowledge, and supervisory background can easily be transferred to your industry.

I would like to come in and discuss this matter with you. I am available any time next week to come in for an interview. If this is not convenient, what times are good for you? If I don't hear from you within 10 days, I will follow this letter up with a phone call.

I look forward to hearing from you.

Sincerely,

Bill Jones

Like Judith Cartwright, Bill Jones is making a major career move and is going about it in a direct and professional manner. The letter is upbeat and to the point. A couple of sentences into the letter he lets his reader know he is making a radical career move, one that is logical and well thought out.

As you can see, the resume alternative letter can be applied to wide-ranging job situations. Whether you're changing career direction or re-entering the job market after a long absence, a properly executed letter can get you in the front door. Remember, the key words are *need* and *focus*. Once you've identified a need and you know you can meet it, the next hurdle is focusing your qualifications and skills on the job in question.

While we're on the subject of letters, let's examine the resume accompanying letter and find out how to use it to good advantage.

nine

Do You Need a Cover Letter?

You feel a lot better now. You've written that first draft of your resume, and you're already thinking about where to send it and fantasizing about the interviews it's going to bring. Hold on for a second. Before you let your imagination run rampant, you're not through yet. You're 75 percent there, but there is one last crucial segment which must be as polished and professional as your resume.

You guessed it. It's the cover letter that accompanies your resume. If you think you didn't need one or that it was an optional afterthought, you're wrong. The cover letter, which may amount to a measly few paragraphs, is an extension of your resume and it also has to be perfect.

Don't think of the cover letter as one last annoying detail. Instead, look at it as the topping on the cake or the hors d'oeuvre before a well-prepared meal. Used in conjunction with your resume, it rounds out and complements your presentation.

Why a Cover Letter?

The best way to answer the heading question is with another question. Can you get away without it? Answer: yes. But you're taking a chance.

Millions of job applicants mechanically mail their resumes out each year without cover letters. It's fast and easy, but not recommended. In this job market, especially, professionalism counts. And the right professional touch is enclosing a cover letter. It may take an hour of your time, but it's worth it.

The cover letter adds a personal touch. In a few carefully chosen paragraphs you're introducing yourself by telling an employer why you're the perfect person for the job. If he wonders why your resume is in front of him, the short introductory letter written on your personal stationery eliminates all doubt. The cover letter immediately anchors you to a specific job and presents you as someone who knows exactly what you're after. As we said in Chapter Five, the cover letter is especially valuable for multi-talented applicants who want to highlight a particular skill and job objective.

More often than not, that little bit of extra effort will have a lot to do with whether you're called in for an interview. As you'll soon see when we get to the chapter on production of your resume, presentation is crucial. The presentation of resume and accompanying cover letter combined is far more effective than that of a resume alone.

Below are some valuable tips for writing your cover letter.

Direct Letter to Appropriate Person

Make sure your letter is sent to the right person. Don't get careless when approaching the finish line and address your letter to director of personnel, or worse yet, the president of the company. How do you feel when you get mail addressed to occupant or resident? You're more inclined to throw it away than open it and read it. So imagine how a poor personnel director feels when she gets mail addressed to her title. It may not be discarded, but it also won't be opened and read with the same enthusiasm it would have received were it addressed to her by name.

All it takes is one phone call to get the name of the personnel director. If the personnel department gives you a runaround, the public relations department will be delighted to help you out.

Open with Strong Lead

Just as your objective on the top of your resume is a terse summation of the job you're looking for, the opening line of your cover letter has to be a grabber as well. Think of the overworked personnel employee at Xerox, IBM, AT&T, weeding through thousands of resumes every year and having to make a preliminary decision as to whether the applicants are potential job candidates. Need I say more? After skimming the 400th resume and cover letter, this person's sense of humor has all but disappeared. Have compassion and make his life as pleasant as possible. By so doing you're increasing your chances of being called in for an interview.

Your opening sentences have to create an immediate rapport and establish your value. They must answer the questions Who are you? and What do you want? Get to the point as quickly as possible. Not with an opening like:

Dear Mr. Holcroft:

Your company is a leading manufacturer of robots, and since I just graduated with a master's degree in robotics, I think I can be of some service. A recent article in *Hi-Tech Age* mentioned that you're always looking for qualified robotics engineers.

But with:

Dear Mr. Holcroft:

The August issue of *Hi-Tech Age* pointed to the pressing need for qualified robotics engineers, and named your company as a world leader in robot output. Having recently graduated at the top of my class with a master's degree in robotics engineering, I know I can make a significant contribution to your company.

The difference between the two openings is obvious. The first is weak, poorly constructed, and rambling. The second example is a little longer, but it commands a stronger tone and paints the applicant as someone who knows what he wants and is not afraid to ask for it. In no uncertain terms, he lets reader know that he knows his field, and is qualified, confident, and ready to assume a responsible position. By mentioning the article in *Hi-Tech Age* in the first sentence, he immediately snares the reader's attention.

In the first example, the applicant mentions the article in the second sentence and begins with a poor opening sentence. The phrase, "I think I can be of some service," portrays the applicant as undecided and unsure of himself. Does he *think* he can be of service or *can* he be of service?

It's no crime to rewrite your opening sentences a dozen times. If that's what it takes to get it right, it's worth every bit of energy you put into it.

Choose Words Carefully

As you can see from the above example, the amount of words you use is not as important as the type of words you choose. The cover letter is only an introduction, a formal handshake if you will. Stick to strong, action words that connote determination, eagerness, aggressiveness, and awareness.

Keep It Brief and Professional

There is no rule-of-thumb as to how many words are needed in an all-purpose cover letter. The cover letter consists of an introduction, explanation, and closing. In total, it may amount to as little as three good sentences, or as much as two to three sentences in each section. However many sentences you use, say what you have to say in a polished and professional tone. Don't be flip, offhanded, casual, or colloquial. Avoid big words. The best letters are simple, unpretentious, and to the point.

Close on Positive/Assertive Note

Along with a strong opening sentence, your letter needs a tight effective close that shows you are serious about getting the job. Don't leave the reader hanging. Mention that you'd like to get together at his/her convenience, you're going to be in town in a couple of weeks, you'd like to set up an appointment, or simply that you'll follow up with a telephone call if you don't hear from the company within 10 days. In other words, make it clear that you intend to take the initiative if you don't receive a response.

Following a few sample cover letters you can use as models.

June 23, 1982

76 Brockport Street
Brockport, Maine 04616
(207) 998-9288

Mr. Carl Denner
Sales Manager
Regents Department Store
22 Havermeyer Street
Brockport, Maine 04616

Dear Mr. Denner:

Thelma Thatcher, eastern sales manager for Crumbley Women's Wear, told me that Regents is opening a downtown outlet featuring moderate to inexpensive women's clothing and will need an experienced sales staff to man it.

It's exciting news for two reasons. First, as sales supervisor for Trower Botley Clothes, I specialized in overseeing the buying for each of the store's five downtown outlets, each of which features a moderate-priced line. And second, the proposed new store will be within walking distance of my home.

I consider myself an ideal candidate for the position of either sales supervisor or regional sales manager. I am going to be out of town next week, but if convenient, I would like to stop in one day the following week and discuss the possibility of joining your growing organization. Meanwhile, until we get together, you can peruse the enclosed resume at your leisure.

If I don't hear from you, I'll call you when I get back from my business trip.

Sincerely,

Ellen Twip

June 21, 1982

90 Lindmart Road
Providence, Rhode Island 02906
(401) 777-2765

Mr. Donald L. Siebert
Siebert, Reynolds, Hodkins, Inc.
7 Wycott Lane
South Providence, Rhode Island 02919

Dear Mr. Siebert:

This letter is in response to your ad for an accounting assistant in the
Sunday *Providence Journal*, June 20, 1982.

I recently graduated from South Providence High School with a straight
B average, majoring in accounting and related business subjects. I have
many of the qualifications you are looking for. As an accounting assistant,
I will be in an ideal position to learn and grow with your company.

Enclosed is my resume, which describes my working experience thus far.
I would like to get together with you as soon as possible to discuss this
position in greater detail.

I look forward to hearing from you.

Cordially,

Timothy Hughes Cartwright

June 29, 1982

98 Elmer Drive
North Caldwell, New Jersey 07006
(201) 228-9962

Ms Eileen Duvale
Sabine & Sabine, Inc.
45 Rockefeller Plaza
New York, New York 10020

Dear Ms. Duvale:

The current issue of *PR Update* mentioned that your company will be
representing Johnson Chemical Co.

Since I specialize in the chemical industry, working in both a copy and account executive capacity, I became very excited when I read the brief insertion. Johnson Chemical is a growing, multinational operation, an account I would like very much to work on.

I am an account executive with Winthrop & Sons, Inc., in charge of three accounts with copy responsibilities for two of those accounts. Winthrop is a solid little company and the accounts are stable and medium-sized. However, after a decade in the business, I want to take on new ground and tackle bigger and more innovative accounts where I can put my public relations experience as well as my knowledge of the chemical/drug industry to good use.

You'll find my well-rounded background perfectly tailored to your company's needs. I'd like to meet with you either at your office or possibly after work to discuss working for your company in a position that taps my account executive and copy talents. The enclosed resume will give you a broader, in-depth perspective of my background and capabilities.

I will call you within the next five days to arrange a convenient time for both of us to get together.

I look forward to meeting you.

Sincerely,

Gloria Hogbrith

ten

Incubating and Test- Marketing Your Resume

Time for a breather. Resist the temptation to go right to the final draft of your resume and letter. You've taken your time thus far to produce a first-rate product. Now go the distance so your resume and cover letter are 100 percent perfect.

This is the time when you're most apt to make errors. Like a runner approaching the last leg of a race, you're about to unleash that last bit of energy so you can dash over the finish line to victory. Try to hold on just a little longer. You can do it. You've been living and breathing your resume for a few days, if not longer. Now is the ideal time to put it aside for a day, preferably a weekend, so you can look at it from a fresh perspective. That's what the incubation and test-marketing periods are all about.

You'd be amazed what time and distance can accomplish. It heightens your awareness, fine-tunes your critical abilities. It's an old journalistic trick. Put copy aside for a couple of hours or even a day when possible, and go back to it. You'd be surprised what you'll find. It's like reading a new piece. All of a sudden, errors, inconsistencies, typos, misspellings, and other miscellaneous items jump off the page at you. You wonder why you didn't spot them before. The reason is you were too close to it, preventing you from being objective.

Not to waste precious time, while your resume is gathering dust, create a checklist chart or use the sample checklist that follows to make sure your resume is complete and you've forgotten nothing.

RESUME CHECKLIST

	Yes	No
1. Name	_____	_____
2. Address & zip code	_____	_____
3. Telephone number & area code	_____	_____
4. Job objective	_____	_____
5. Work experience section complete?	_____	_____
6. Education (dates, degree(s) attained)	_____	_____
7. Affiliations	_____	_____
8. Special skills	_____	_____
9. Personal data	_____	_____
10. Information accurate (names, dates)?	_____	_____
11. Technical terms and descriptions accurate?	_____	_____
12. Grammar correct?	_____	_____
13. Any typos?	_____	_____
14. Have you repeated yourself?	_____	_____
15. Can sentences be shortened or tightened?	_____	_____
16. Have you left anything out?	_____	_____

After your resume has incubated for a while, read it over and check the appropriate box to make sure you've left nothing out.

What did you discover? I bet you made some changes, tightened a few phrases, found an inconsistency or misspelling that passed you by before.

Was your resume worth incubating?

Now to the final draft. This is the last draft before you type it (or have it typed) on clean white paper. You're in the homestretch, just a step away from printing it.

Test-Market Phase

Once the final draft is completed, read it twice slowly to see if you can pick up any errors. At this late stage, you can expect your copy to be just about perfect.

As a last precautionary step, give your resume to a couple of people to see what they think of it. Not just anyone, but someone who can render a constructive opinion—a business associate, relative, or good friend. You never know, someone may pick up an error made consistently throughout the different stages, or spot an inconsistency that might turn a prospective employer off. But more probably you'll be congratulated on turning out an award-winning resume.

Don't just take one person's word. To be absolutely certain, get a couple of opinions. Then you can rest easy and finally put your resume into production. How shall we produce it so it looks positively smashing? What options are open to us? Let's find out.

eleven

How Important Is Production?

First impressions count. They count when you meet someone for the first time, and they certainly count when a personnel director is skimming through a stack of resumes piled high on his desk. No matter how brilliantly you constructed your resume and how qualified you are for the job you applied for, if your resume doesn't look good, it will not get an objective reading.

"Not fair!" you scream indignantly. If you've forgotten, think about overworked personnel employees in corporate offices all over the country. Out of a stack of 500 resumes, do you expect your resume to be given special attention if it was run off on an ancient mimeograph machine that produces smudged and sloppy-looking copies?

Be Your Own Art Director

Just as you were copywriter/editor/proofreader during the writing process, now it's time to try on your art director's hat for size. You have just as much leeway in typing, laying out your resume, and printing it as you did when you wrote it. You can take a number of paths. Your goal is not to produce a resume that looks like a magazine cover, but simply one that is neat, clean, easy to read, and, above all, professional-looking.

Setting Up Your Page

Before your resume is typed, decide how your copy is going to be laid out. On a blank piece of paper, pencil in one-half inch margins around the entire page. The page will be a working model of what your actual page will look like. Within the margins, determine how many words can fit on a line and how many lines will fit comfortably on a page, with heads and appropriate spaces. It doesn't have to be exact. The idea is to have a guide as to how your copy will fall on the page. Next, lightly write in your headings the way you'd like them to appear.

For variety's sake, move your headings around to see how they look in different positions on the page. If you don't want to erase a heading each time, make a couple of sample dummy pages so you can play around and arrive at a copy arrangement that pleases you.

Don't go with the first layout you try. Try your headings flush left, flush right, or centered throughout the page. Still not satisfied? Try underlining them. Instead of doing all your headings in capital letters, use upper- and lower-case letters and then try underlining them. Better? Take a look at the sample pages here.

_____

_____

_____

_____

Objective: _____

_____

_____

Summary: _____

_____

_____

Work History: _____

_____

_____

_____

_____

_____

Education: _____

_____

Personal: _____

_____

_____

_____

_____

_____

Objective

_____

_____

_____

Experience

_____

_____

_____

_____

_____

_____

Education

_____

_____

Affiliations

_____

Personal

_____

_____

_____

_____

Objective

_____

_____

_____

Experience

_____

_____

_____

_____

_____

_____

_____

_____

Military

_____

Education

_____

_____

Personal

_____

Should You Type It Yourself?

It depends. First, can you type? You don't have to be a professional typist to type your own resume. But you do have to be accurate, neat, and keep errors down to a low roar. You can white-out an occasional error. But if your resume is awash with white-out marks, you're taking chances. If you're not careful, too many corrected errors can discolor the page.

If you're not comfortable with a typewriter, have a professional typist do it. It's not that expensive and your resume will look first-rate.

If you type it yourself, don't use any typewriter. Since the resume will be printed, it needs a firm, dark, clean impression. Generally speaking, portable manual typewriters can't guarantee a consistent imprint throughout the page, whereas a decent electric typewriter (IBM, Olivetti, Royal, etc.) will turn out a clean page that will reproduce well.

As for type style, avoid typewriters with fancy typefaces. Script type, for one, is not appreciated by personnel workers. And an elite typeface, while acceptable, is small and hard to read. Ideal is the pica typeface.

Some applicants opt to have their resumes typeset. It looks great, but it's also expensive and unnecessary. Most personnel people couldn't care less whether your resume was typeset or not. Save your money.

What Kind of Paper?

Keep it simple. Avoid fancy expensive papers and thin fragile ones that crinkle as soon as you touch it. An absolute no-no is colored paper. You're not going to impress a personnel worker with a resume printed on pink, baby blue, or grass-green paper. Off-white, buff, and light tints are acceptable. To be on the safe side, stick to solid white paper. It prints well, looks good, and will be well received.

How Should It Be Printed?

In the past you could get away with photocopying your original resume and sending a copy to each job you applied for. Not any longer. The job market is a lot more competitive now, and it's also a lot more particular. One sure way to turn a prospective employer off is to send a photocopy, or worse yet, a carbon copy of your original resume. This late stage is no time to economize. You've turned out an excellent product thus far, now go the distance and produce something you can bet on. It's not that expensive to have your resume printed. Whatever the cost, it's worth it in the long run if it improves your chances of being considered. Three common duplicating processes are multilith, mimeographing, and photo-offset.

Multilith is not expensive and produces a clean, professional-looking copy. Mimeographing is cheap, fast, and not recommended. Schools and small companies use it for running off newsletters and inexpensive publications. The final product is often uneven and discolored. In the end, you get what you pay for.

Photo-offset, like multilith, turns out good-looking copies. Its only drawback, however, is that it can be proportionately more expensive than multilith if you're printing a small number of copies. Photo-offset is recommended if you're printing over 200 copies.

A word of advice. Printing prices vary dramatically. Don't go with the first printer you speak to. Comparison-shop and make sure you're getting your money's worth.

In the long run it pays to have a reliable, reasonably priced printer you can count on. You're going to be using him several times throughout your career. Six months down the road, you may have to have more copies of your resume run off, or possibly a new resume printed. What about personal stationery?

An easy way to find a good printer is speak to friends or business associates. They'll be happy to steer you in the right direction.

That's it. Your resume is completed and you're ready to launch a frontal attack on the job market. Before we outline some resume strategies and job-hunting tips to make life easier, a few words on resume services, multiple resumes, and revising your resume.

twelve

How Good Are Resume Services?

Leaving this chapter for the last segment of the book was not an act of sadism on my part. It was done purposely. If you intend to use a resume service, you could have bypassed the first 11 chapters and started right here. Or you could have saved some money and not purchased this book. That would have been a mistake.

Yes, you can have a professional resume service prepare your resume, and many of them do first-class work. You're paying for it, and like anything else, the more you spend the more you get (most of the time, anyway). Many executives pay hefty prices to have their resumes written and produced.

Disadvantages of Resume Services

A good resume service will do everything short of hand-delivering your resume. A professional resume writer takes down all the pertinent career information, and a couple of days later you receive a draft, which gives you a chance to add, delete, and edit. Once final copy is agreed upon, your copy is typeset, and finally printed on good paper. Doesn't sound bad, does it?

Before you get excited, consider some of the drawbacks of using a resume service:

Formula presentation. A resume service will guarantee a professional product and that's what you'll get. Bear in mind, however, you're getting a formula resume. Despite what resume services tell you, they're applying proven formulas to create saleable resumes. More often than not, they rely on cliches and stock techniques to turn out hundreds of resumes every week. To the harried resume writer who is taking down all your career information, you're one of many clients, and as soon as you leave his desk, you'll be reduced to an inanimate mass of numbers, facts, dates, and jobs. Even though your resume looks like it can snare an award for its sparkling graphics, it lacks a vital, intangible element—your personal touch.

Can be expensive. Resume services are not cheap. Most of them work pretty much the same way. A consultant spends up to an hour and a half with you taking down all the resume information, and depending upon the amount of work entailed, charges you a fee for 100 copies (standard amount). The fee ranges from $100 to $250 and includes consultation, writing, editing, typesetting, and printing. Smaller shops pride themselves on churning out resumes in assembly line fashion. Their price for a one-page resume can range from $75 to $100, and if there is a second page, there is an additional $25 charge. A few resume services promise 24-hour service. Most, however, will give you a finished product within three to five days.

On a grander scale, there are job consulting firms or services which promise to do everything from evaluating your skills, finding the career area you'll excel at, writing and producing your resume, to launching a job search campaign that results in a good job. In other words, they do everything. All you have to do is pay the bill, which can run up to thousands of dollars, depending upon time and services provided.

I'm not going to evaluate these consulting outfits. Suffice it to say, some are expert at what they do, others are less than reputable. It's important to know what you're getting into before you make an appointment. Some offer a free consultation before they mention signing a contract and subsequent costs. No matter how you look at it, it can be an expensive proposition.

Advantages of Doing It Yourself

Writing your own resume is not only cheaper, but there are other advantages to consider. First, it's a valuable learning experience. Along with mastering resume writing techniques, which can easily be applied to other types of writing you'll be doing later on, you're also pinpointing saleable skills and personal traits, information that will be on the tip of your tongue during a tense interview. Second, you're developing disciplined job-search skills which you'll profit from throughout your working life.

Nobody says resume writing is fun. But consider what you're taking from the experience. By writing and designing your own resume, you're fully in charge of your job search campaign. You're not relegating any part of it to an impersonal third party. At a later date, when it's time to amend, update, or revise your resume, you won't have to depend on a resume service, or anyone else for that matter, to do the job. You'll be able to do it all yourself.

thirteen

How Many Resumes Do You Need?

One all-inclusive resume does the job for most job applicants. Yet many of us boast a number of saleable skills. If you fall into this latter category, one resume highlighting all your skills can sometimes do more harm than good. There is such a thing as overkill, giving too much information, thus confusing a personnel person who might dub you over-qualified, or even unstable. Obviously, being so labeled is going to do little for your job search.

Highlight Pertinent Skills

Don't present information that might be construed as conflicting or that paints you as being all over the map. If you're an experienced advertising person with copywriting and account executive skills, it's best to separate the two job functions when applying for a job in either capacity. If you just lost your job as an account executive and you're applying for a new job as chief copywriter, play up your copywriting capabilities and minimize your account executive background. Don't leave it out of your resume alto-gether, but discreetly push it backstage. Highlight only what best sells you. Ideally, you should have two resumes on standby at all times, one for copywriting jobs, another for account executive jobs.

Don't forget what we said about marketing your resume. For a bull's-eye reaction, your resume has to be targeted to a specific job. If your career spans three decades, and you're competent in a few areas, three separate resumes might be even better than two.

Generally, accountants, attorneys, comptrollers, business managers, technicians, etc., find that one resume can be used for most jobs in their respective fields. But public relations workers, advertising people, journalists, communications specialists, and even engineers often discover that one resume doesn't do them justice.

It's not easy preparing two or more resumes on yourself. The question is how to best sell yourself if you have two skills and have worked in two allied job areas (such as copy and account executive work in advertising).

If you are applying for a job as a public relations writer, for instance, and your background consists of magazine as well as public relations jobs, the easy way out is to drop all magazine experience from your resume. Be careful! That approach can easily backfire. What about the time gaps in your resume? All of a sudden, a personnel director discovers a two-to-four-year time gap where you did absolutely nothing. More dangerous is extending the period worked in public relations to cover the time you worked in magazines. What if a personnel worker calls your past employers for an evaluation of your employment record. One call and it's all over. An innocent white lie can cost you a job you were seriously being considered for.

A practical marketing strategy is having two resumes, one for public relations jobs and another for magazine jobs. Both resumes contain a lot of the same information, the difference being one sells you for public relations jobs and the other for magazine jobs. It's just a question of creatively playing off your skills and honing in on the ones you want to highlight. The difficult part about writing two resumes is selectively editing out information not pertinent to the job you're applying for.

Let's look at the following sample resumes of Carol C. Dwight, who has performed both advertising copywriting and account executive functions. Since most advertising people do a fair amount of job hopping, on short notice she might apply for either a position as copywriter or account executive. Note how the two resumes are constructed.

Carol C. Dwight
243 Edgemere Street
Tenafly, New Jersey 07670
(201) 333-8765

Objective
To secure a challenging position with a growing advertising agency where I can use my copywriting skills to best advantage.

Work Experience

Brown, Bain, Wilson & Henry, New York City, Copywriter, 1976–present.
As copywriter for this medium-size agency, I organized a detailed advertising strategy for Forbart Cosmetics' new line of toiletries. Formulated

initial concept and wrote copy to match. The copy presentation, which included a series of radio and television spots, resulted in a monthly sales gain exceeding 25 percent. Monitored program closely, making sure client and agency were satisfied throughout the campaign.

O'Connor, Hyle and Digby, New York City, Copywriter, 1972–1976.
Wrote all copy for the Wooley Cosmetic line, an expensive line of fine perfumes, lipsticks, and toiletries. Since this is a major account of the agency's, I worked closely with the company's vice president in designing and finally writing copy that was satisfactory to company's senior management. As this is an old-world conservative company, I was careful to create a copy program that maintained and clarified the company's unique industry position.

Bell & Gantler Advertising, New York City, Copywriter, 1970–1972.
Part of large advertising staff, I functioned in a subordinate status as third person in a six-person copy staff. Helped create, design, and write advertising campaigns for three of firm's clients. Initially, I worked in a backup capacity, developing ideas of the other copywriters. Just six months after I started I submitted concept and copy for a three-stage advertising campaign that involved print and radio exposure for DeMain Perfume. Copy was accepted by copy chief the day I submitted it and was approved by the company the next day. From that point on, I was encouraged to develop my copywriting talents.

(etc.)

Carol C. Dwight
243 Edgemere Street
Tenafly, New Jersey 07670
(201) 333-8765

Objective
To secure a challenging position as an account executive with an agency with an expanding account base in the cosmetics industry.

Work Experience

Brown, Bain, Wilson & Henry, New York City, Account Executive, 1976–present.
This medium-size agency specializes in cosmetics accounts. With a staff of three under me, designed $3 million campaign for Forbart Cosmetics' new line of toiletries. Once campaign was successfully underway, resulting in monthly sales gains of over 25 percent, I worked closely with company's executive staff to make sure agency was meeting their needs. Acted as buffer between client and advertising firm and was also responsible for major copy changes.

O'Connor, Hyle and Digby, New York City, Account Executive, 1972–1976.
Was second in command over the prestigious Wooley Cosmetic line, an expensive line of fine perfumes, lipsticks, and toiletries. As this was a

major account of agency, maintained daily contact with the company's vice president in charge of promotion. Since I was the agency's company liaison, better than 20 percent of my time was spent on the road, shuttling between client's subsidiaries, their Chicago home office, and the agency.

<u>Bell & Gantler Advertising, New York City, Account Executive Assistant, 1970–1972.</u>
Part of six-person staff. Helped create advertising campaigns for three of firm's clients. Once campaigns were organized and copy approved by copy chief, worked closely with head account executive, maintaining close weekly contact with each of the accounts, making sure they were supervised properly.

This is one way to market dual skills. In the enclosed samples Ms Dwight cleverly mined her talents. She didn't fabricate, and she left no gaps in her resume. All she did was selectively edit. In applying for an account executive's job, she discreetly played down her copywriting background, and in applying for a copywriting job, she honed in on her writing talents.

Many job applicants are not aware that they can present themselves in different ways. An attorney who has a strong background in tax work and real estate law might do better with two resumes, one highlighting his tax background, the other, real estate. A systems analyst who has a sales and systems analysis background could also profit from two resumes.

The questions to be answered are, Do you need more than one resume? and Does having more than one improve your marketability? Let the specific job situation dictate whether it's necessary.

fourteen

How Often Should You Revise Your Resume?

Don't make the mistake of throwing out your resumes, resume files, and worksheets when you land that special job. I know how you feel. The job search is finally over and you think you won't need them any longer. So why not toss it all in the wastepaper basket and forget about it.

Resist that temptation. You'll regret it and curse the day you threw all your hard work away. The smart person keeps his/her resume handy and up to date just in case. In this job market, you never know when you may have to activate your resume on a moment's notice.

What if a business associate in a competing company calls and says there is an opening at his company for a person of your skills and background. The person who held the job was fired suddenly, and for some unknown reason the company has to fill the spot immediately. "Get your resume over here pronto," he whispers into the phone.

If you're in tune with today's job market, your resume is in a convenient file at home. It needs a little updating, but since there is no time to revise and print new copies, you opt to tack on an addendum, bringing your work history up to the present.

In emergency situations like the one mentioned above, a resume addendum, which amounts to a couple of paragraphs describing your present position and job functions, is perfectly okay. A resume that tracks your background to the present is better.

But what if you didn't have a current resume? You know what that means? What with the responsibilities of a full-time job, it could take you a full week to get a new resume written, edited, and printed. By that time other applicants will have gotten their foot in the door, and if the company is in a mad rush to hire someone, a rival candidate with credentials that don't match yours will be in the wings waiting to see the president of the company.

Better Safe Than Sorry

The above scenario is not farfetched. It happens every day and great opportunities are lost because many of us are not prepared to move on a moment's notice. Face facts: If you were to leave your job right now, there are at least 2,000 applicants who can sit in your swivel chair and do the job as well as you. All these candidates are ready to spring into action if given the signal. Their resumes are prepared, their suits neatly pressed, and they're capable of charming the birds from the trees if they have to.

Don't forget the ground rules. Before you fantasize about becoming president of your company and eventually retiring and enjoying a fat pension 25 years down the road, understand that you could be pounding the pavement if your company falls on hard times; you're a victim of reorganization, merger; or by some bad stroke of luck, you're fired. Situations change, you change, your job functions change, and due to circumstances beyond your control, you have to move on to greener pastures.

Stay Current

If your resume is current and your files are in order, revising your resume shouldn't give you an anxiety attack. The trick, however, is to stay on top of the situation and not get sloppy. It's very easy to lose track of time and let two or three years slip by without giving your resume a second thought. If that happens, the revision process becomes a lot harder. The longer you wait, the more work you have to do. Wait five years or more without updating your resume and you may have to start all over again. Avoid that if you can.

Every time there is a significant change in your work status, make note of it and include it in your resume file. If you are promoted, given a new territory and responsibilities, or move to a new division, make sure it's properly recorded in your resume file, along with backup information, dates, and details. If your reorganization plan was accepted and resulted in a 50 percent increase in company sales, all the support data should automatically find its place in your file. You'd be surprised what can happen within a 12-month period. You might be promoted from lowly clerk to supervisor, changing your whole perspective on life. All of a sudden, you're earning more money, you have more responsibility, and you have an exciting future ahead of you. All these pertinent details have to be duly highlighted in your resume file.

When to Revise

The $64,000 question is, How often should you revise your resume? With up-to-the minute records at your disposal, the revision process poses few problems.

Some applicants routinely revise their resumes every year: others, who work in volatile industries, do it every six months. Knowing the characteristics of your industry and company, you'll have to come up with a system that works for you.

To avoid printing a new resume once or twice a year, an alternate plan is to have an updated, edited draft on standby at all times. You can update it as often as needed, and if the need arises, you can have it typed and printed within 24 hours.

Out of the clear blue, you too may get a call from a friend or business associate, telling you about a fabulous opportunity you'd be foolish to pass up. It could happen tomorrow, even today. Are you prepared?

fifteen

How to Use Your Resume

You're holding that perfect resume in your hand and you're justifiably proud of it. Now what? Whatever you do, don't flood the market with it. Would you be embarrassed if you mistakenly sent your resume to the same firm twice, even three times? It happens every day. Routinely, job applicants respond to the same blind ad a number of times without realizing it. Aside from cluttering a personnel worker's desk with multiple copies of your resume, you're also wasting time. When it's essential you find a job quickly, there's not a second to waste. Each resume you send out has to be carefully targeted. The best way to accomplish that is by tracking your resume with a resume log. They're easy to set up and maintain and essential for a thorough job search.

Consider the sample log that follows.

RESUME LOG

	Date	Company Address	Person/ Title	Response Date	Follow-up	Interview	Comments
1.							
2.							
3.							
4.							
5.							
6.							
7.							
8.							
9.							
10.							
11.							
12.							
13.							
14.							
15.							
16.							
17.							
18.							
19.							
20.							
21.							
22.							
23.							

By using the log religiously, you'll know where you are at every moment. Each time you send a resume out, make an entry on the chart, filling in the date sent, company, person you sent it to, etc. What could be simpler? When you get a response, positive or negative, make the appropriate entry. If you make a follow-up call, note that as well. Later on, your interviews and comments can be recorded as well.

In the beginning of your job search, it may seem like a big waste of time. "Why keep a log?" you'll complain. "I know where I sent my resume." True enough in the beginning. But what happens when you have over 50 resumes scattered among companies, recruitment firms, and employment agencies? Are you going to remember where you sent each one, when you sent it, along with follow-up data, names of contacts, and comments? If you're lucky enough to have a photographic memory, you'll have no problems. Unfortunately, most of us are not blessed with that heightened faculty. Take it from people who have launched successful job campaigns. They'll tell you how important it is to have a tight system, one that gets your resumes to the right places and moves you speedily along until you capture the job you stalked.

Now let's find out where to send the resumes. In Chapter Two I touched on the importance of checking out the terrain, creating systems, and setting up charts for organizing an effective job search campaign. Let's go one step further and find out exactly where to send resumes for the best response.

Field Study

Know where the jobs are in your occupation. Without realizing it you probably have a pretty good grasp of your field. You may already subscribe to trade magazines covering it, which can be a valuable source of information. In the back of many trade magazines are a couple of pages of classified advertising listing jobs around the country, even abroad.

Spend some time in your library and look through *Standard & Poor's Directory of Corporations* and the *Encyclopedia of Associations. Standard & Poor's Directory* lists the addresses and chief operating officers of most publicly held firms, along with the company's products and sales and revenue figures.

The *Encyclopedia of Associations* lists all the trade associations throughout the country. Maybe you aren't aware of it, but your field has an association that will be delighted to provide you with a wealth of information. A call to the association's publicity director can result in ideas, salary information, and possibly some job tips.

Employment Ads

The employment ads in your daily newspaper give you a good indication of the current job picture. There are three broad categories of ads: company, agency, and blind ads. All of them can be useful if you know how to use them. Count the number of ads listed covering your field. They will give you a clear idea of what the job picture is like and help to structure your job search campaign. If there are a couple of pages of ads for your specialty, it means there are plenty of jobs. But if there are just a few ads, take the hint and carefully plan your approach. Generally speaking, the job market is tight and highly competitive. Get into the habit of keeping close watch on the employment section of your newspaper. It's an easy way to get a capsulized view of the job prospects in your industry. Traditionally, Sunday is the most important day for employment advertising. This is when the readership is heaviest and when the majority of ads are published. Wednesday is another favorite time among agencies and employers for running employment ads.

Company ads. Company ads leave nothing to the imagination. Typically, they are straightforward ads listing qualifications and educational background desired and even ball park salary figures. At the bottom of the ad, the company asks for a resume and sometimes a cover letter telling something about yourself and why you want the job. Also included is the personnel director's name and company address.

Employment agencies. Employment agencies can be valuable, but it depends upon the agency. Not all employment agencies are going to be right for you, and many won't give you the right time of day, much less a lead on a good job.

Find out which agencies service your field. The Sunday employment section of your newspaper tells you this at a glance. Beyond responding to ads that interest you, make note of the agencies that specialize in your field. Even though they are not advertising jobs that meet your qualifications, it doesn't hurt to stop in, register, and leave some copies of your resume. You never know.

Agencies earn money by getting applicants jobs. You pay nothing, the agency bills the company. It's not hard to understand why placement managers are constantly under the gun and operating at fever pitch. The more applicants they place, the more they earn. Hence, the negative term for them: flesh peddlers. Cruel, but true. However, a conscientious placement manager might turn your life about and get you the job you dreamed about.

Also keep in mind a busy employment agency can resemble a railroad station. Don't get discouraged, don't spin on your heels and leave. People file in and out all day long, and it's not uncommon for a placement manager to forget you as soon as you leave his desk. Knowing this, make it your business to stay on top of the situation.

If a placement manager tells you she's sending your resume out to a company, don't wait for her to call you. Three or four business days later call to see if there is news. The best way to work with an agency is to stay current. Maintain weekly contact until you know where you stand.

Be careful when registering with several agencies servicing your field. Without realizing it, multiple copies of your resume may wind up on the same personnel director's desk. This is to be avoided. As a rule, employment agencies are reluctant to tell applicants where they send their resumes. But if you tell them you're registered with a couple of agencies, they'll have to respect your wishes and say where they're sending it. If they won't comply, find another agency.

It's quite common for a company to list a job opening with several agencies. Be careful.

Blind Ads. Watch out for blind ads. They also appear frequently in the employment section of your newspaper. They're like any other employment ad, except they don't identify the company by name. Instead of sending your resume to a company, you're responding to a post office box number.

Some employers use only blind ads. What with a rising unemployment rate and a job market glutted with applicants, blind ads are becoming increasingly popular. The obvious reason is anonymity. Small- or medium-size companies that don't want to be bombarded by phone calls from job-starved applicants can go about their job search in privacy. Blind ads also permit unscrupulous employment agencies that have no openings to quietly scour the market to see who's looking for work; they're merely window-shopping for talented applicants for future jobs.

On the flip side, blind ads can create problems for the job seeker, namely, anxiety, uncertainty, and on occasion, embarrassment. Not knowing where your resume is going can make anyone uptight; you don't know whether it is at a blue chip, second-rate, or slipshod operation. Finally, since you don't know where or to whom your resume is going, it could even wind up on your boss's desk, if he just happens to be looking for an addition to the staff, or worse yet, your replacement if you're on the brink of being fired. If you're not careful, responding to the wrong blind ad can backfire in your face and cause no end of grief.

What precautions can you take? Be careful which blind ads you respond to. Read them carefully. If an ad sounds remotely familiar, is poorly written, or has little concrete information about the job, don't respond. Reputable companies provide complete job descriptions, and you shouldn't have to guess what the job is all about.

On your resume log, keep track of the blind ads you respond to, listing the post office box number and distinct features of the ad in your comments column. You never know when you may spot the same ad. It doesn't hurt to be cautiously skeptical.

Executive Search Firms

Both executive search firms and employment agencies provide applicants with jobs. The difference lies in the approach and the type of jobs they specialize in. Employment agencies work directly with applicants, whereas executive search firms deal exclusively with companies. An employment agency earns money only if they place an applicant, whereas a recruitment firm is paid a fee by the company whether or not they find someone a job. Lastly, recruitment firms concentrate on placing applicants in executive posts, which usually start at salaries of $30,000 and go all the way up into the stratosphere. Naturally, the higher the salary, the larger the fee the recruitment firm earns for the placement. Also, the method of recruiting applicants is a bit more sophisticated. A major recruitment firm finds applicants by several methods, ranging from personal contacts, trade journals, trade association contacts, advertising, and the corporate grapevine.

sixteen

Job-Hunting Tips to Consider

Finally, keep an eagle eye on the job market at all times. Whether you're comfortably employed or eagerly looking for that special job, never lose touch with the job market. The astute job seeker monitors the market carefully, almost scientifically. Nothing is left to chance. He doesn't wait for an opportunity to knock; he creates his own opportunities. Even when you're comfortably situated in your plushly carpeted office with a majestic panoramic view of your city, don't get too comfortable and lose your sense of objectivity. No matter how secure you are, be on guard. You never know when the wind will turn and you'll have to empty your desk and move on to greener pastures. Unexpectedly an alarm may sound and your job search campaign will have to be activated.

Operate from Position of Strength

The strategy-minded job seeker operates from a position of strength at all times. If things turn sour on her present job and she sees that her days are numbered, she doesn't wait for the ax to fall. Before her corporate American Express card is canceled, she's on the phone telling her printer to run off 100 copies of her resume.

Once her resume and stationery are on press, the job search campaign moves into high gear. She knows time is of the essence. From past experience, she knows it's prudent not to leave a job until there is a new job to replace it. That's a basic job-hunting commandment. Don't try to analyze the psychology behind it, accept it as fact. An employer deems you more valuable and a hotter property if you're employed, rather than "on the street" looking. You're an applicant with potential, someone who is leveraging your way to a stronger, more powerful position. Not only do you appear more valuable, but you're also in an excellent position to negotiate a substantial salary increase. Whereas, if you're out of a job, an employer has you in a subtle hammerlock, and depending upon how desperate your situation, will do his darndest to get you as cheap as possible.

Whether you're currently employed or looking for a new position, use both the conventional job-hunting strategies outlined in previous chapters and your own private network of contacts to uncover job leads and information.

We began this book discussing the importance of job-hunting strategies, and we're going to close on that note. Beyond employment ads, employment agencies, and executive search firms, each of us can create a private web of contacts that can be a rich source of career information. If mined properly, they can eventually lead to the job of your choice. Let's find out more about networking procedures.

Networking

No one knows for sure who coined the word "networking." The process of using friends, business acquaintances, and referrals to uncover job leads originated with women's groups in the mid-70s. The purpose of the women's networks is to provide career information for women entering the work force at all levels. It eventually led to the formation of formal job clinics, workshops, and symposiums in wide-ranging fields.

Networking is not new. Job applicants have always relied on friends, family, and business associates for job leads. What is new, however, is that more and more job applicants are forming systematic networks of contacts and referrals.

You'd be surprised how valuable a network can be. Through a network, people you know can help you find a job. Your network of contacts becomes a resource you can tap.

Let's set one up. Start with a basic working list of 20 friends, acquaintances, business associates, relatives, past employers, and authorities who may be able to help with your job search. Once your names, addresses, and telephone numbers are in front of you, decide which ones you know well enough to call and which ones it's more appropriate to send resumes and cover letters to.

Just as you set up a resume log in Chapter Fifteen, to insure accuracy and avoid duplication in creating your network, use the following network log to accurately track each contact.

NETWORK LOG

	Date	Person	Address	Response	Comments	Lead
1.						
2.						
3.						
4.						
5.						
6.						
7.						
8.						
9.						
10.						
11.						
12.						
13.						
14.						
15.						
16.						
17.						
18.						
19.						
20.						
21.						

Remember, you're creating a web, or network, of contacts. It's a process requiring time and nurturing. Every name on your list is not going to materialize into a lead. However, don't be discouraged. Your original list of 20 names may quickly whittle down to five or six names, possibly fewer. But in the process of paring your list, you also have the opportunity to expand it and add new contacts to your network. A blind alley may uncover a fruitful lead, which may mean an interview. As your network expands and becomes more complicated, you're making inroads in your job search. The exciting thing about a network is that it creates a snowball effect all by itself. One call or letter leads to something else, and all of a sudden, you're sitting on a couple of hot job prospects.

Once the foundation of your network is formed, it becomes stronger each year. The wise applicant has his pulse on the marketplace at all times and makes sure his network is intact and constantly working for him. As you move along in your career, meet new people, join organizations, travel, your resource network gets tighter and more resilient. Eventually, you'll hear of job leads, openings, promotions, who's hiring and who's firing, not through the classified section of your newspaper or an employment agency, but through a resource network you've put together yourself.

No matter what system you use, make sure you're one step ahead of everyone else. Building a solid career foundation is important. Yet in these hard times, you have to have something else working for you. Living in the present is not enough. Smart job seekers occupy two worlds. One part of themselves is thriving in the present, the other is getting ready for what's ahead. They're ready to accept and adapt to change as it occurs. They're in harmony with themselves and the world around them. All their job-seeking skills are honed to the marketplace. Their resumes are perfect, they've mastered the game, they look and act like ideal job candidates, their interview rapport is flawless. Add a positive, assertive attitude and they'll have everything they want in life—and more.

appendix

Sample Resumes

LIBRARIAN

Brenda Lopilo
89 Cypress Court
Oakland, California 94607
(415) 445-9926

Objective
Senior librarian working in a research and consulting capacity.

Book Acquisition
Purchase books and other materials to maintain library that meets needs and interests of public.

Update Catalogues
Classify materials for general and specialized readerships. Conduct educational programs, such as community projects, public affairs, creative arts, and youth forums for inner-city youths.

Supervise Young Adult Section
Assist elementary, junior, and senior high school students with selecting and using books and other library materials. Organize projects and programs, such as book and film discussions, and also coordinate library projects with school programs.

Assist School Librarians
Routinely meet with school librarians concerning new developments and systems for coding and processing books and information. Instruct school librarians about new methods for familiarizing students with library's resources. Prepare lists of materials on assorted subjects and help select materials for school programs.

Work Experience
1970–Present, Project Coordinator/Senior Librarian, Fremont Public
        Library, Oakland, California
1965–1970, Librarian, Riverside Public Library, San Francisco, California
1961–1965, Librarian, Egmont Library, San Francisco, California

Education
Stanford University, Bachelor of Arts, 1958
University of Southern California, Master of Library Science, 1960

Foreign Language
Speak Italian fluently

Affiliations
Ten-year member of Librarian's Society of America

Personal
Married/two children

PLANT FOREMAN

Edward Holder
87 Dolan Drive
Middleton, Michigan 48856
(517) 888-9965

Objective
Plant foreman of large automotive manufacturing company

Work Experience

1970–Present, ABC Spark Plugs, Cedar Falls, Michigan, Plant Foreman
Started as assistant day-shift supervisor in charge of crew of 250 workers divided between assembly line functions and bench operations. Made sure work quotas were met and took over for supervisor when sick or on vacation. Within three years was promoted to day-shift supervisor, and two

years later was promoted to night foreman. As night foreman, initiated incentive work programs where workers received pay differentials for increased output during lobster shift. Program was successful as lobster shift output increased by 75 percent. Because of success of night incentive program, management asked me to formulate similar program for day shift in order to increase productivity.

1962–1970, Jackson Automotive, Middleton, Michigan, Shift Foreman
Medium-size company manufactures and distributes wheel bearings. As shift foreman I alternated between monitoring day and evening shifts. Maintained rigid work quotas and also acted as intermediary between union shop steward and company production executive. In last three years with company, responsible for instituting quality control system whereby worker output can be more thoroughly evaluated.

1960–1962, Chase Foreign Car, Middleton, Michigan, Shop Foreman
Chase is the largest foreign car repair shop in Middleton. Services all foreign cars and maintains two shifts. Responsible for overseeing crew of 30 mechanics. Made sure cars were logged in, logged out, and production schedules kept. At end of day, kept charts on mechanics' repair schedules so they could be evaluated on a monthly basis. Every six months, recommended key workers for promotions and raises. Authority to hire and fire new workers to meet demanding production schedules.

Education
Middleton Vocational High, vocational diploma, automotive trades, 1958
Kingsbridge Community College, associate degree in diesel and fuel-injection automotive systems, 1960

Personal
Married/three children

EDUCATOR/SUPERVISOR

Jim Hardwich
9 Cromwell Place
West Greenwich, Connecticut 06836
(203) 873-8825

Career Objective
A teaching/supervisory position working with emotionally disturbed and retarded children where I can put my 17 years of teaching experience to good use.

Work History

1975–Present, Teacher/Supervisor, Elmont Elementary School
Hired to put together experimental teaching and counseling program for emotionally disturbed and retarded children. Pilot program began with 10 youngsters and within a year grew to include 30 children with assorted

problems. With two assistants, devised structured program consisting of classwork and counseling sessions so children could be integrated into school system and eventually into real world. Initially school authorities were doubtful about system, but I convinced them that integrated school setting is the most effective and stimulating teaching environment. The children, with problems ranging from mild to severe, prospered and performed well. The program is still in operation, although it has expanded to accommodate 150 children.

1970–1975, Teacher/Special Education, The Fremont School of West Hartford
This small private school has special education program consisting of two classes, one for severely disturbed children and another for those with mild learning disabilities. Shaped curriculum for both classes. The program for the severely disturbed child consisted of part classwork and counseling, and the curriculum for the mildly learning disabled was an integrative educational approach which paralleled school curriculum, although at a slower pace. Both were deemed successful as I was able eventually to integrate 85 percent of my students. Also counseled parents so they could work with children at home.

1965–1970, Teacher/Elementary School, The Greenwich School
Taught first, second, and third grades. Excellent learning experience because it allowed me to hone my teaching skills while I went to school at night preparing to move into special education. Taught the three Rs, and did some off-hours' counseling work with children who needed special assistance. Experience proved good groundwork for next teaching assignment.

Education
New York University, bachelor's degree, School of Education, 1965.
Columbia University, master's degree, psychology, 1968 (special course-work in working and teaching the disturbed child); graduated with high B average.

Personal
Married/no children

CHEF

Betty Alton
76 High Road
Los Angeles, California 90042
(213) 778-8210

Objective
Chef in medium to large restaurant featuring continental cuisine.

Continental Menu
Well versed in all aspects of preparing a balanced continental menu. Can take a basic American cuisine and turn it about and create dishes prepared

in a French, Italian, Spanish, or German style. Concoct wide-ranging sauces to create interesting, versatile, and offbeat dinner menus. Equally comfortable working with fish, foul, beef, and pork. Specialize in creating attractive and reasonably priced menus featuring exotic fowl, such as quail, goose, pigeon, and capon.

Nouvelle Cuisine
To meet demands of current culinary tastes, mastered a complete nouvelle cuisine menu featuring interesting fish and fowl dishes, sparked by light sauces and nonfattoning vegetable creations.

Menu Preparation
Long-range menu preparation. To take advantage of good market prices, work at least three weeks ahead in purchasing staple products. Having worked at restaurants seating between 150 and 300 guests, can accurately plan food budgets and prepare menu so I'm operating within budget and able to forecast what profit margins will be in an average week.

Purchasing
Responsible for purchasing all food for a restaurant. Adept at taking advantage of sales, and getting excellent prices for food. Meat, fish, and fowl are purchased at market each day, whereas other items are purchased a week to two weeks in advance. Keep accurate charts of food expenditures and changing prices, and am careful to structure budgets so a significant profit is realized.

Supervision
In charge of as many as eight chefs along with an additional five- to ten-person staff maintaining kitchen on daily basis. Hire and fire chefs as needed, monitor production of each chef, and responsible for each chef's individual creations.

Employment
1975–Present, Le Soir Restaurant, Head Chef, San Francisco, California
1972–1975, The French Table, Supervising Chef, Los Angeles, California
1968–1972, Bon Appetit, Chef, Los Angeles, California
1965–1968, Albert's, Chef, Los Angeles, California

Education
University of Southern California, two years, courses in food preparation and food management, 1963
Culinary Institute of California, studied nouvelle cuisine and French baking, one-year curriculum, 1964.

Personal
Married/one child

CARPENTER

Lloyd Harrison
24 Maitland Avenue
Detroit, Michigan 48236
(313) 667-9655

Objective
Carpenter specializing in rough and finished work. Specialty is building exterior foundation work in new houses and custom cabinet work.

Experience

1978–Present, Head Carpenter, DeVries Construction Co., Detroit, Michigan
Large construction company responsible for approximately 35 percent of the residential construction in downtown Detroit. With three senior and two junior carpenters, we alternately worked on two houses at a time. Mornings were spent building wood foundation from blueprints. Houses ranged from three- to four-story houses to ranch and split-level houses on one to two acres of land. In afternoon, concentrated on finishing all wood-work in houses where wood and brick foundations were built. Answered to chief project foreman. Adhered to rigid time schedules and materials and employee budgets.

1974–1978, Carpenter, Columbo Construction Inc., Detroit, Michigan
Company specializes in interior office construction in downtown Detroit. Once building was completed, six-person carpentry crew built all cabinet work from architect's blueprints. Depending upon the office, I worked with a variety of woods, building desks, shelves, and custom furniture.

1972–1974, Cabinetmaker, Jones Cabinets Ltd., Detroit, Michigan
Small shop concentrated on contract work for residential housing market. To contractor's specifications, built chairs, desks, shelving, and kitchen cabinets. Worked in traditional woods along with the more difficult cedar, redwood, mahogany, and special pines. Precision work requiring care and advanced carpentry skills.

Training
Three-year apprentice program with Local 5 of Carpenter's Union; included classroom instruction plus two years on-the-job training
Graduated top of class from Carpentry Trades High School in Detroit, 1971.

Personal
Married/one child

Harold Fuller
89 Cromwell Avenue
Chicago, Illinois 60610
(312) 876-9977

Objective

Entry-level training position in commercial or savings bank leading to managerial position.

Work Experience

1972–Present, Commercial Teller, Chicago Bank & Trust

After a three-week training course, worked closely with experienced teller for additional two weeks before I was competent enough to work on my own. In course of normal day, transacted different types of accounts and alternately worked loan and bond window and savings/checking account window.

1970–1972, Teller, First Chicago Trust & Savings

Four weeks of extensive training at savings window and I was functioning on my own for the remainder of my stay with bank. Part of alternating staff of 20 tellers, shifting between check-cashing, special transactions, and savings window. In last year with bank, manned special window for reconciling complex transactions for overseas accounts.

Education

Majored in business administration at Illinois Business Institute, two-year course, 1969. Graduated with business and commercial diploma from John Eltwood High School, Cedar Grove, Illinois, 1967

Personal

Single

MANAGEMENT/RETAIL JEWELRY

Jeanne Pinto
22 Ardmore Avenue
Knoxville, Tennessee 37914
(615) 787-9988

Objective
Management and supervisory responsibilities in retail jewelry outlet.

Employment History

1975–Present, Jewelry Manager, Hayes Department Store, Knoxville, Tennessee
Operated store's successful jewelry section. Specialized in wide variety of jewelry, from imported costume to expensive hand-crafted pieces made of

bronze, brass, and gold. Promoted retail outlet by having showings of talented jewelry makers. Over five-year period, increased sales 75 percent.

1972–1975, Manager, Jewelry Centers, Inc., Knoxville, Tennessee
Supervised five large jewelry concessions throughout city. Assisted in buying jewelry which ranged from moderately priced to expensive. Hired experienced salespeople to man concessions located in department and clothing stores. Monitored sales, and made sure each concession featured a unique display of jewelry that appealed to customers at that location. Created sales incentive program whereby salespeople earned commissions if they sold a certain amount of jewelry per week. Helped boost sales on a weekly basis by approximately 45 percent per employee.

1968–1972, Jewelry Buyer, Fashion World, Knoxville, Tennessee
Responsible for buying all jewelry for major clothing store. Initially, jewelry section was small and operated by one salesperson. Instituted new buying program which introduced new jewelry makers and broadened line to include expensive jewelry in gold and silver. Sales increased by 95 percent during first month. Hired three new salespeople, and jewelry department began to make a significant contribution to store's sales. Steadily increased line until it was a leading showcase for talented jewelry makers throughout area.

Education
Graduated Knoxville University, bachelor's degree, retailing, 1968

Personal
One child

HOSPITAL ADMINISTRATION

Laura Botbine
96 Hoshkins Road
Dallas, Texas 75209
(214) 662-0114

Objective
Middle-management administration position in large urban hospital.

Work Experience

1975–Present, Assistant Administrator, Victory Hospital, Del Rio, Texas
Responsible to administrator with direct authority over purchasing and hiring and firing of lower-echelon workers. Responsible for creating yearly budgets based upon thorough analysis of profit and loss statement. Over five-year period maintained tight reins over yearly expenditures, and kept yearly budgetary increments at less than 10 percent. Working closely with personnel department, made sure clerical and technical staff worked to capacity and pared overtime expenditures over a four-year period by 35 percent.

1970–1975, Assistant Administrator/Purchasing, St. Helena Hospital, Dallas, Texas
In charge of purchasing budgets for all departments of this large urban hospital. Department heads submitted budgets for approval and after careful analysis of cost accounting sheets, created budgets that did not impair profits and that kept pace with inflation.

1964–1970, Assistant Budget Director, Mountainview Hospital, Dallas, Texas
Assisting head of purchasing department, gathered information and data for annual budget planning reports. From my analysis of costs and expenditures against current profits, yearly budgets were meticulously mapped out. Analyzed data and did studies comparing Mountainview's expenditures to that of hospitals of similar size.

Education
Bachelor of Science, Business Administration, Houston University, 1962; straight B average throughout.

Personal
Single